A Small I
Doing I
the Inte

A Small Business Guide to Doing Big Business on the Internet

Brian Hurley
Peter Birkwood

Self-Counsel Press
(a division of)
International Self-Counsel Press Ltd.
Canada   U.S.A

Printed in Canada

First edition: February 1996; Reprinted: August 1996

Canadian Cataloguing in Publication Data
    Hurley, Brian, 1961-
    A small business guide to
    doing big business on the Internet

    (Self-counsel business series)
    ISBN 1-55180-029-2

  1. Business enterprises — Computer network resources.
2. Internet (Computer network). 3. Information networks.
4. Internet advertising. I. Birkwood, Peter, 1958- II. Title.
III. Series.
HD30.335.H87 1996   650'.0285'467   C95-911105-0

Survey results quoted on pp 10-12, 15, 66, 67, 86, 118, 126,
and 133 are copyright 1995 by Georgia Tech Research
Corporation. All Rights Reserved. Source: GVU's Third
WWW User Survey (http://www.cc.gatech.edu/gvu/user_sur-
veys/) .

Cover photography by Terry Guscott, ATN Visuals, Vancouver, B.C.
Cover props courtesy of Vancouver Maritime Museum,
Vancouver, B.C.

Self-Counsel Press
(a division of)
International Self-Counsel Press Ltd.

1481 Charlotte Road   1704 N. State Street
North Vancouver,   Bellingham, Washington
British Columbia V7J 1H1   98225

Contents

Tables

Figures

Acknowledgments

The authors would like to thank their wives, Rima Felfli Hurley and Patricia Birkwood, for their support and patience with our many long evenings, weekends, and holidays used in the preparation of this book.

We would also like to thank Roger Hill, Dirk Tempel, Paul Birkwood, George de Witte, David Brewer, Michel Pedneault, and our wives for their review and comments on our draft manuscripts.

A special thanks to Natasha Young, Ruth Wilson, and Judy Phillips of Self-Counsel Press who made the production of this book an enjoyable and satisfying experience.

We dedicate this book with love to our children, Erin Birkwood and Brandon Hurley.

Brian Hurley
bhurley@magmacom.com

Peter Birkwood
birkwood@magmacom.com

Introduction

There has been a great deal of excitement in the international media over the significant commercial potential of the Internet. Much of this excitement has included fanciful discussions of cyberspace, virtual reality, romanticized computer hackers, glittering information "highways," fabulously profitable on-line commerce, and new high technology trends that will lead to better lives. When U.S. president Bill Clinton sent his first electronic mail message in March 1993, it sent a signal to the world that the White House saw the Internet as a key element of the new information age and as a new way of doing business. Many commercial enterprises stood up and took notice, and they are now viewing the Internet as a significant element of their business operations. Small, medium, and large businesses are now trying to understand the benefits, perils, and practical steps they should be taking to get on-line in order to take advantage of this unique environment.

What is the Internet? In brief, it is a worldwide computer network that uses the telephone network to interconnect over 160 countries with electronic mail and 92 countries with the full suite of electronic services detailed later in this book. Essentially, users dial into a secondary computer, known as a *host computer*, to access the available Internet services and information repositories on other computer sites.

The Internet, which began as a scientific network sponsored by the U.S. military in the early 1970s, has grown to today's network of over 4.8 million host computers connecting more than 30 million users. This phenomenal growth is fueling speculation by industry pundits that there could be 100 to 150 million users by the year 2000.

Since the early 1990s, commercial enterprises have eyed the Internet as a potentially viable means of advertising, selling, and supporting their products globally. As of 1991, the number of commercial networks registered to connect to the Internet exceeded the traditional academic, scientific, and military users, indicating the strong trend toward commercial use. Worldwide, there are now over 50,000 access networks connected to the Internet backbone communications environment. These networks contain millions of individual personal computers, engineering workstations, and mainframe computers. The National Science Foundation (NSF), the U.S. government agency that has guided the evolution of the Internet, has published the demographics of companies requesting Internet addresses as follows: commercial (51.3%), research and development (28.7%), government (8.9%), defense (7.1%), and education (4.0%).

As evident from these statistics, commercial enterprises already dominate the Internet and are playing an increasing role in its evolution. The NSF has recognized that the natural evolution of the network is toward commercial applications and has consequently lifted restrictions on commercial use of the network.

The Internet certainly represents exciting technology to the computer enthusiast, and as a consequence, most material that has been written to date has been largely technical in nature and focus. To the businessperson, however, the Internet primarily represents another technology tool which may help achieve the business's main goal: greater profitability.

This book has been specifically written for business people who want to make use of the Internet to enhance their existing business enterprises or create a new distribution channel for their products or services. The book specifically focuses on Internet service opportunities that may be used to form the kernel of a new business or enhance an existing one.

As with any new business, the keys to success lie in knowing who your customers are, identifying what types of products and services they would find valuable, and making your product or service easy to buy and use, as well as creating cost and operation structures that will lead to a healthy bottom line. An Internet-based business is no exception to these well understood rules of thumb. The businessperson needs to understand the nature of Internet technology options so that time and investment capital are spent wisely.

Today, businesses are using the Internet in many different ways to improve their day-to-day operations. The potential for on-line sales of products and services is one of the major reasons businesses are attracted to the Internet. There are currently many companies that have already improved their bottom line and increased sales using the Internet as a global point-of-sale terminal. The allure for the entrepreneur is that you can —

- provide easier and more direct access to your company;

- sell products seven days a week, 24 hours a day, with a significant on-line sales potential to a global market;

- direct on-line marketing and advertising to millions of connected consumers;

- reach all of your on-line customers to electronically notify them of a sale or promotional event;

- build a clientele and develop customer relationships electronically;

- increase the effectiveness of internal and external business communication with customers and suppliers, including the transfer of e-mail and data;

- provide on-line product support globally;

- electronically survey the customer base, or receive customer suggestions on ways to improve your product line or service, any time;

- provide effective product and after-sales support;

- eliminate at least a portion of your costly paper-based advertising and marketing expenses (and help save the environment at the same time);

- save on the cost of full-time salespeople;

- work out of your home, saving on store operating costs;

- update your product catalogues electronically so that prospective customers always have the latest information;

- go global without the cost of setting up offices in foreign countries; and

- compete on a par with the large corporations since no one knows how big you are when you are on the Internet.

On-line shopping currently represents only a tiny percentage of the estimated $73 billion a year catalogue shopping industry. With estimated receipts in the order of $50 to $200 million, on-line shopping represents a mere 0.25% of the total industry. The current market trend, though, is for both home and business computer users to become increasingly connected to the Internet and other on-line networks that allow for greater customer control, product selection, and product variety. If this trend continues, and a modest 2% to 5% of the catalogue shopping market goes on-line, it will represent sales of $1.46 to $3.65 billion per year.

On-line shopping is commercially very important but is not the only type of business that can exist on the Internet. Many types of information services exist, including financial and investment advisories, reference libraries, special interest interactive discussion groups, travel and leisure information, electronic communication services, games and entertainment services, and news, weather, and sport summaries. In addition, there are also many Internet-based service provider opportunities that support the operation of the Internet itself.

This book has been structured to help you assess whether or not the Internet represents a good business opportunity for your existing or new enterprise. Each chapter has been structured to answer a specific business question as part of this assessment.

Chapter 1 answers the question "What is Internet technology and who are its users?" It provides you with an overview of the potential customer base and its demographics. Chapter 2 deals with the question, "How do I access the Internet?," while chapter 3 discusses the Internet tools, allowing you to develop familiarity with their functions and helping you determine which tools you may want to use.

Chapter 4 provides an overview of various resources you can use to find files and sites on the Internet. Chapter 5 is a step-by-step guide to planning an Internet-based business so that customers will have a clear understanding of the nature of the product or service being offered. A seven-step business analysis process is outlined and can be used to establish your business objectives, financial commitment, as well as provide relevant legal and security information which can be included in a formal business plan.

Chapter 6 deals with the questions "How should I offer my product or service to my customers over the Internet? How can I use the Internet to improve my existing business communications infrastructure?" Chapter 7 discusses nontraditional business opportunities on the Internet: opportunities for the entrepreneur that exist because of the Internet itself.

Chapter 8 focuses on addressing the operational details of running your electronic business including advertising and marketing the product, getting subscribers signed up, selling and distributing the product, handling credit card verification in a secure way, handling product returns and problems, and streamlining the billing process.

The question of whether you should purchase Internet services from a third-party provider or whether you should consider operating your own Internet service platform is discussed in chapter 9.

Chapter 10 focuses on the future of the Internet and on-line market forces that are causing the telecommunications network providers to support a more sophisticated Internet. This information will be useful in helping you map out a three- to five-year business plan in this rapidly changing marketplace.

We have also included an appendix of recommended reading for the curious Internet entrepreneur, and a glossary of Internet terms.

Note: All figures throughout the text are in U.S. dollars unless otherwise stated.

1.

The Internet and its users — an overview

Understanding the Internet from a business perspective requires some knowledge of on-line electronic services in general, Internet-user demographics and characteristics, methods of getting Internet access, and Internet technology and tools.

What are on-line services and how do they relate to the Internet? You will need to understand the differences between the various options since they tend to attract and cater to different types of people.

Understanding Internet technology and methods of access is important so that you can intelligently determine the tools needed to implement your business service in the most efficient way possible. This knowledge will also prove valuable if you wish to talk to any one of the on-line service providers about how your business could fit into its service environment. Common language helps to create a common understanding of the business problem to be solved.

Please take the time to read this chapter carefully; it will greatly increase your understanding of the potential of the Internet service opportunities available to you.

a. The Internet: What it is and where it comes from

Different people see the Internet in different ways. Some comments people have made about the Internet are that it is a great educational and learning tool, a cornerstone of democracy and freedom, a cultural experience, a network of computers that allows unfettered communication, a huge business opportunity, the foundation of the "information highway," and a confusing lot of technobabble.

While all of these statements have varying levels of truth, the Internet is really simply a collection of computers interconnected by high-speed telephone lines. The personal contributions of the network users and the software tools deployed on Internet computers are what create the network's unique characteristics. When the Internet was first conceived, it was for very practical purposes. Military and academic personnel in sites across the United States needed a means to efficiently communicate with each other on a day-to-day basis about the government projects on which they were working. Efficient communication had three main requirements. Participants wanted to be able to: informally exchange electronic letters between two or more people on the project; ship project data files between two computers; and use a remote computer from a computer terminal so that valuable computing resources could be used by distant users.

The term "Internet" comes from the concept of "internetworking," which simply means allowing two or more networks to connect together. One of the principle beliefs of the original founders of the Internet was that no single large network could ever satisfy the needs of all users. The Internet architects concluded that the ability to connect or "internetwork" networks of different types and sizes was a more practical scenario and hence a key design requirement. To the user of this vast interconnected network, however, the Internet had to appear as one single network, the underlying computing and communication technology complexity hidden from view.

This vision of simple user access and flexible network connectivity proved to be farsighted. Today, a business can purchase personal computers (PCs) for head office, connect them via a local area network technology, and exchange electronic mail (e-mail) or data files with its branch offices by connecting over the Internet. The same business can use the Internet to conduct both internal and external business with this same access connection. Today, there are globally over 50,000 different commercial, government, education, research and development, and defense networks "internetworked" in this fashion.

Based on NSF 1995 statistics, Canada ranks as the most connected nation in the world per capita (150 networks/million population), followed by Australia (110 networks/million population), and the United States (87.5 networks/million population, with California ranked as the most connected U.S. state, at 169 networks/million population). France, the United Kingdom, Germany, and Japan follow, in that order.

Over the last several years, much of the development on the Internet has centered on helping the user navigate more easily electronically, and find information on products and services using new search and display tools. These powerful Internet software services often have funny names, such as Gopher, Telnet, e-mail, Veronica, Archie, WAIS, World Wide Web (the Web), and many others. Most industry experts agree that the popular explosion of the Internet, beginning around 1993, has

---

Business tip:
Company activity on the Internet

Some Internet statistics can be misleading if you don't know where they come from. An often-quoted statistic of a measure of commercial activity is the rate at which *domain names* are being registered to connect to the Internet. Domain names are the portions of an electronic address unique to that company over the entire Internet. Companies must register the domain name with a central Internet organization that administers all addresses. Many companies in the United States and Canada have jumped to register their unique names for trademark or corporate recognition reasons without actually activating these new domain name addresses on the Internet (i.e., not allowing people to communicate to the new address).

The measure of how many companies are active on the Internet versus those that have domain names but are not active is a statistic that is unknown. Interestingly, organizations in the United Kingdom are required to activate their domain names at the same time as they register them to prevent misuse of Internet address space.

been primarily due to user-friendly Web tools that have opened up the Internet to virtually everyone, and made it as easy to use as "point and click." Such software packages have also encouraged business enterprises, from the Fortune 500 companies to small home-based businesses, to set up shop on the network. Over 20% of Internet traffic as of April, 1995, was users on the Web. This traffic figure was 0% only two years earlier. Clearly, many commercial enterprises are taking full advantage of Web technology to tell the world about their products and services.

A question often asked is, "Who pays for the Internet?" The short answer is that everyone who is connected to it does. You pay your Internet service provider (ISP) to be able to access the Internet. Your local ISP may pay another larger service provider for its Internet access. The large provider provides interconnection between cities and with other similar, competing large ISPs. In the past, this large provider was typically a government-funded facility and in some countries, still is.

In the United States, the role of the large ISP was played by the NSF. Until recently, the NSF funded the telecommunications facilities that were the core of the Internet. However, in 1995 the NSF stopped supporting these facilities and turned them over to private companies. Today, anyone wanting to access these facilities must pay a fee for connection.

There are a number of companies that have set up as large ISPs, and they meet at locations called hubs, where Internet traffic can pass between the networks. The NSF still funds some of these hubs; however, this is also expected to end sometime in the future. The NSF also maintains responsibility for administering the Internet domain names, and charges a fee to register and own domain names it administers (with some exceptions).

The various "free" resources on the Internet, such as Web sites, databases, and public file archives, are provided by the owners of other computer systems connected to the Internet. Many Internet resources are provided by educational institutions as a service to support research and education. Other resources are provided by business concerns in an attempt to attract visitors to their on-line presence or to build goodwill.

Business tip:
Being neighborly in an electronic community

An electronic community is a group of people who socialize and interact primarily through an electronic medium (e.g., real-time discussion groups, newsgroups, or e-mail). For example, some Usenet newsgroups are considered an electronic community, as are some BBSs, such as Whole Earth 'Lectronic Link (The WELL). Electronic communities tend to adopt group norms and, just like "real" physical communities in cities, have both real and implicit rules of behavior by which users of the electronic services abide. Failure to follow the real rules can lead to your losing your access privileges, and failure to follow implicit rules of behavior can lead to exclusion and harsh criticism.

For a business, it is important to note that electronic communities represent demographic groups. An awareness of the nature of an electronic community will ensure that you are targeting individuals who are potential customers. It is also important to note that a business that fails to understand the existence of real and implicit rules of an electronic community puts itself at risk of alienating customers rather than attracting them.

b. Electronic on-line services

Getting access to the Internet from the home or business may have been a problem in the past, but it is not an issue any more. There are three main classes of service providers which will give a user the desired access. These are the Internet service providers (ISPs), commercial on-line service providers (OSPs), and bulletin board systems (BBSs).

What is the difference between these three types of service providers? While each may provide Internet access, there are different business and technical perspectives that each addresses.

1. Internet service providers (ISPs)

Users can access the Internet directly from their home or office computers through normal telephone lines via an Internet

Canadian nationwide ISPs

Advantis Canada
i STAR
HookUp Communications
Integrated Network Services Inc.
WorldLinx Telecommunications
UUNET Canada Inc.

U.S. nationwide ISPs

AlterNet
Global Connect
internetMCI
Netcom
Portal Information Network
Performance Systems International

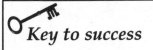

Key to success

Freenets provide no-cost Internet access

Freenets have sprung up all over the Internet. They are a service provided by many regional non-profit institutions which give the general public free access to Internet e-mail services. Freenets are extremely popular because of their no-cost access to Internet resources. All you have to do is register with the institution to get a password and user ID. However, users may have difficulty connecting into a computer site that everyone else is also trying to access. Freenet administrators generally limit users to short sessions to allow other users time on the system. Local governments are also taking advantage of freenets to disseminate information to their constituents.

service provider. *Internet service provider* can refer to any company that provides Internet services, or it can refer to a company that specializes in Internet services only. Commercial OSPs and BBSs may fit into the first category but not the second. In the case of a specialized ISP, there are user-pay versions and there are *freenets*, where the user doesn't have to pay for the Internet access. By far, most ISPs are the paying kind, freenets typically being provided by nonprofit organizations as a service to the community.

ISPs are also referred to as *Internet access providers*. (Unless there is a need to differentiate, any company that provides Internet access is referred to in this book as an ISP. We also differentiate between OSPs and ISPs as required.)

An ISP may be an informally maintained system run by a teenager or it may be run by dedicated professionals as a commercial business. The ISP generally charges a flat rate per month, which covers a minimum connect time, and then a per-time rate, which is charged once the minimum connect time is used. These services typically provide the user with e-mail, registration services for Internet network addresses, a choice of Internet-connection methods, Internet-access software for PCs, Macintoshes, or UNIX-based workstations, access to a news server, and user helpline support. In addition, many ISPs now provide Internet training, consulting, and other services to allow companies to set up shop on-line.

2. On-line service providers (OSPs)

Users may also access the Internet indirectly through a commercial on-line service provider such as CompuServe, Prodigy, America Online, Delphi, GEnie, ATT Interactive, and Microsoft Network. These commercial *on-line service providers* (OSPs) are professionally run businesses that supply paying subscribers with access to a wide range of information-, entertainment-, and merchandise-oriented services on their own private network. Almost all of these companies are now offering Internet-service access as well as their own service portfolio, since they see Internet as a way of enhancing their own business and providing a broader service offering to their subscriber base. Many of these companies were originally set up to capitalize on the information services and on-line shopping market trends, and were funded by private-sector market demands, in contrast to the Internet which was originally government funded. Typical OSP services include the following:

- News, sports, and weather summaries
- E-mail
- Reference libraries
- On-line shopping
- Financial and investment information
- Travel and leisure information
- Games and entertainment services
- Special interest group discussions
- Internet access
- User helpline support
- Special Internet access software for PCs and Macintoshes

As a customer, you pay for an account that allows you to connect to the service provider's computer system. While the OSPs have different charging schemes, all usually involve a monthly subscription fee and some form of time or per-service use fee. In addition, there are often many extra charges for special services added to the user's monthly bill depending on usage.

The OSP originates many of the on-line services that it provides, but also acts as a broker for other companies that contribute specialized services, such as financial databases. If your business is considering setting up an electronic storefront or mailbox on an OSP network, you must carefully look at the rate structures and rules enforced by the service provider relative to customer use of your on-line account. Some OSP charges are based on how many messages you send and on how many messages you store locally, and have different rates depending on whether the message arrived from the Internet or was internal to the service provider's computer network. In general, for simple Internet access, it is more expensive to subscribe to OSPs than it is to ISPs.

3. Bulletin Board Systems (BBSs)

A *bulletin board system* (BBS) is also an OSP but with a number of differences. BBSs are generally much smaller than OSPs — with a subscriber base in the thousands or tens of thousands per

OSPs providing toll-free, on-line access from major metropolitan areas

- America Online: 4,500,000+ subscribers
- CompuServe: 3,000,000+ subscribers
- Prodigy: 1,200,000+ subscribers
- Microsoft Network: 200,000+ subscribers
- Delphi Internet Services: 100,000+ subscribers
- GEnie: 75,000+ subscribers
- Apple eWorld: 65,000+ subscribers

BBS, versus hundreds of thousands or millions of subscribers per OSP — and also more numerous than OSPs (it is estimated that there are around 150,000 BBSs in operation). As well, BBSs are more informal and more transitory than other OSPs, since the investment to set one up is relatively small. BBSs are also more local to towns and cities, since they generally don't have nationwide toll-free access, and generally run on PCs, versus mainframes for the large OSPs.

Typical types of services that BBSs offer include:

- Discussion groups
- Conferencing
- Document search and retrieval
- Fax on demand
- Real-time chat
- Electronic entertainment
- E-mail
- Computer files for downloading (e.g., games, applications, pictures)
- Internet access (it is estimated that 60% of BBSs have Internet access)

Although there are examples of large BBSs that come close to matching the services offered by the larger OSPs, most are geographically limited because most customers don't want to pay for long distance charges. Some BBSs provide toll-free or high-speed data access, but this is the exception rather than the norm because of the cost of the service and the small subscriber base.

The Internet provides a cost-effective way for existing BBS providers to compete on a global basis. The main factor limiting BBSs from offering full Internet access is that an expensive PC software or hardware upgrade is required in order to reap the full benefits of the Internet. BBS software vendors are scrambling to match the demand, and in 1994 and 1995 they announced new versions of software in an attempt to keep their products competitive.

Large, popular BBSs with reaches that exceed their local geographical boundaries include The WELL, Channel 1, and Software Creations Bulletin Board System. These three BBSs all have Internet access. The WELL distinguishes itself because it has developed into an electronic community and has a large and regular subscriber base. Software Creations BBS distinguishes itself by being a central distribution point for outstanding entertainment-oriented shareware software.

Business tip:
Internet as a level playing field
for small business

The differences between BBSs, OSPs, and ISPs are diminishing. The large OSPs may be in for some interesting competition in the near future, since the Internet is larger and more diverse in content than any of the on-line services, and many comparable Internet services don't have any usage charges. In areas where the OSPs offer per-usage services, opportunities exist for entrepreneurs to specialize and offer a better service — eating away at the OSP customer base.

This leveling of the playing field is due to two main factors. First, the penetration of Internet into the consumer market makes it a viable connection medium for an increasing number of potential customers who were previously geographically limited because of expensive toll charges. Second, the reduced cost of powerful PC hardware and software is enabling the average businessperson to compete on an equal footing with the large OSP computer networks.

---

c. Who uses the Internet?

Knowing who your customers are is one of the cornerstones of a successful business enterprise. The following questions, then, must be answered:

(a) Who are the Internet users?

(b) What are their backgrounds?

(c) What motivates them?

(d) What kind of computers do they use?

(e) Do they have money to buy products?

(f) How and where are these users accessing the Internet? For example, are they using e-mail only or do they have access to more sophisticated text or graphics tools like Gopher, WAIS, or the Web?

(g) Are they accessing the Internet through a BBS, OSP, or an ISP?

Three very useful Internet-user surveys were conducted on the Web by the Graphics, Visualization and Usability Center at the Georgia Tech Research Corporation (GTRC) between January 1994 and April 1995. Another survey included some collaborative work with the Hermes Team at the University of Michigan Business School on consumer issues related to the use of the Internet. These surveys, conducted using a volunteer method, attempted to characterize the Internet user and determine the demographics of this community at large.

A word about Internet surveys: statistics and surveys can be misrepresented, and it is popular to challenge the techniques used by those conducting the survey. Most surveys performed by nonprofit organizations are organized around getting Internet users to voluntarily contribute personal information through survey instruments set up on Web sites. This method has been frowned upon by some people as not being statistically valid.

Nonetheless, the GTRC information represents a good cross section of the Internet community. Previously, no real data existed on Internet demographics; this information represents the best available to date. These surveys provide reasonable data points to start your business analysis; keep your eyes open for ongoing published information on this subject as it becomes available through future surveys.

The GTRC surveys found that the Internet community is composed of highly educated, predominantly white, North American males in their mid-thirties who have money to spend and are computer literate, though women are rapidly becoming a larger component of the Internet demographic picture. PCs and Macintoshes have become the predominant computers accessing the Internet, in contrast to the predominance of UNIX workstations found in the first survey.

Predominant operating systems accessing the Internet*

- 52% PC Windows
- 26.2% Macintosh
- 8.8% UNIX
- 13% Other

Prodigy Users:

- 86.5% PC Windows
- 13.5% Other

*GTRC 1995 survey

The 1995 GTRC survey also found that the majority of Internet users worked in the computer industry (31.4% of all users), followed by those in education and professional fields (23.7% and 21.9%, respectively). Management trailed at 12.2%. Of the users surveyed, over 67% said that they were willing to pay fees for information services, providing quality was ensured.

According to the survey, over 70% used network browsers at least once a day, and 50% spent two to six hours each week in front of the computer, exploring the Internet. Almost 46% of respondents said that they explored the Internet for more than six hours each week.

Separate statistics published by OSPs indicate similar results to the GTRC surveys. Prodigy-user information provides a view of the differences between users subscribing to an OSP and those subscribing to Internet through an ISP. Prodigy on-line statistics indicate that Prodigy, a commercial on-line service provider, has 1.2 million subscribers, the typical subscriber being a 41-year-old, married professional with a household income of $72,600. Membership statistics indicate that of its total population, 61.6% are male and 38.4% female. About 30% of households log on once a day, and the typical subscriber uses the service 8 to 11 times a month, with the average session time being 14 to 16 minutes.

CompuServe, with a customer base of three million subscribers, has a whopping 92% male membership and 8% female membership. Statistics indicate that 3.8% of all trips to the CompuServe-run electronic mall result in a sale, with an average on-line purchase of $65 to $70. CompuServe has over 170 electronic advertisers, varying in products and services from Brooks Brothers, Columbia House, Ford Motors, McGraw-Hill, and JCPenney, to companies selling computers, office supplies, financial services, electronics, hobby supplies, housewares, and health and travel services.

BBSs are also a popular access medium, with an average on-line life of three years. Each BBS averages 469 regular callers, 344 paying callers, and 98 new callers per month. Most BBS users are attracted to the software, entertainment, and discussion groups which they can obtain locally.

Differences in the capabilities of the software tools that users have will affect the strategy your business can use to focus

---

Reasons for using the Internet*

(Respondents answered more than one category, causing total to be greater than 100%.)

- 82.6% Browsing
- 56.6% Entertainment
- 50.9% Work
- 32.6% Academic research
- 10.5% On-line shopping

*GTRC 1995 survey

marketing and sales effort in reaching these customers. Understanding where the users access the Internet from will help you map market demographics of your customers.

GTRC survey results indicate that Internet access is divided among primary internet providers as follows: local on-line providers (e.g. ISP's, BBS's) 27.9%, major on-line providers (e.g. Prodigy, CompuServe) 27.5%, educational providers (e.g. university) 26.5%.

---

*Average income of Internet users**

- $69,000

Prodigy Users:

- $80,000

**GTRC 1995 survey*

2.

Internet access

This chapter provides a brief introduction to what it means to have access to the Internet and the basic options available.

a. Plugging your computer into the Internet power plant

The Internet may seem imposing to the average person because of its technical complexity. In many ways, however, the Internet and its relationship to computers can be considered analogous to the common household electrical outlet. When you plug your toaster into the wall socket, you can make toast without having to understand electrical theory. The Internet is similar in that you can plug your computer appliance into the Internet network socket, but you receive information rather than electricity.

In order to use the "electricity" of the Internet, you need a plug that fits the outlet and you need to be using an appliance that matches the voltage of the outlet. To access the Internet, you also need to have an outlet to plug into.

The ubiquitous Internet "appliance" is the PC. There are three basic ways that a computer can be "plugged" into the Internet: through dial-up modem connection, dedicated dial-up modem connection, and leased-line connection. The equivalent of the power plants are the large number of global interconnected computer systems that provide the information resources to the Internet: OSPs, BBSs, or ISPs. There is no shortage of companies willing to provide you with Internet access. ISPs can be found by looking in almost any PC magazine or your local Yellow Pages. (Specific information on how to select an ISP is provided in chapter 9.)

b. *What equipment is necessary?*

Anyone who owns a PC, data communications software (like ProComm, Telix, or CrossTalk), and a 2400 baud/2.4 thousand bits per second (Kbps) or higher modem can purchase a shell account on an ISP and have access to every Internet application. You would not be able to take advantage of any multimedia features of the Internet, but you would be able to access everything else. This type of access is regularly used by thousands of people who interact with the Internet through freenet community services.

If you want to take advantage of the integrated graphical and multimedia capabilities of the Internet, you will need a high-end PC (minimum IBM PC 386, 33 Mhz, 4Mb RAM, 40Mb hard disk), a 14.4 Kbps modem (28.8 Kbps modem preferred), and Internet-capable application software to support a SLIP/PPP dial-up connection.

Modems may be purchased from any local computer store, usually for less than $200. Modems are relatively straightforward to connect to your computer if you follow the instructions.

c. *Access speed*

Access speed translates to delay for Internet users: the faster the link — the greater the bandwidth — the less time spent waiting for the information to arrive. Raw access speeds are difficult to picture in a physical sense when viewed at a numeric level. To help put access speed into perspective, the following table shows approximately how long it would take to send the entire text of this book between two computers connected by a communication link at the various access speeds. Greater bandwidth indicates greater data-carrying capacity.

Speed (Kbps)	Time to send (minutes)
2.4	33.0
9.6	8.0
14.4	6.0
28.8	3.0
56.0	1.4
1,544.0	0.05

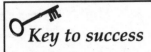

Key to success

Consider your customers' capabilities

If you plan to use graphics and multimedia features on the Internet, be aware of performance limitations of older-model computers. The capability of your customers' computers will limit your customer base if you present your business using a tool that requires a high-performance computer.

The type and speed of connection chosen for business applications should be based on your specific information needs and the Internet services you use. The speed of the connection has a direct impact on the usability of the specific Internet tools. If you have set up a Web server on the Internet, the higher your bandwidth, the quicker your information will be made available to potential on-line customers, and the more on-line customers your site can serve simultaneously.

As well, the bulk of ISP charges for dial-up connections (discussed below) are based on the length of connect time. Therefore, the connection speed also has an impact on the cost. As a dial-up user, the greater the bandwidth, or speed, the less your on-line usage charges will be, since you will spend less connect time than you would using a lower bandwidth connection to do the same work.

Of the three basic connection types (discussed below), a dial-up modem connection is the method favored by casual Internet users, with 14.4 Kbps being the most common access speed. Today, most new PCs are sold with built-in 14.4 Kbps modems, ensuring that this will be the predominant access speed in the near future.

d. Economical access when needed: Dial-up modem connections

For dial-up connections — if you want to connect to the Internet on a casual basis — all you need is a modem. Dial-up modem access is useful because it allows you to use only as much Internet connect time — the length of time that you are connected to the Internet access — as you need, when you need it. It also allows you to make use of the telephone line for other purposes when the computer is not connected to the Internet. However, dial-up accounts do not guarantee that you will always be able to connect to your ISP when you want to. The dial-up lines that provide access to ISPs are available on a first-come, first-served basis; during peak periods, it could be difficult to connect, which may not be acceptable to some businesses.

The next step upward from dial-up modem access, in terms of cost and improved availability to the businessperson, is *dedicated dial-up modem access*. This is the same as dial-up modem access, except that your ISP dedicates a telephone number to you, and the dial-up line is always available for as long as you want.

Internet users and their connection speed *
- 43.7% 14.4 Kbps modem
- 13.1% 10 Mbps (ethernet)
- 12.0% 28.8 Kbps modem

Prodigy users:
- 73% 14.4 Kbps
- 20% < 14.4 Kbps

*GTRC 1995 survey

When it comes to cost, dedicated dial-up access is significantly more expensive. Dial-up access may be purchased for $20 per month or less from an ISP. Dedicated dial-up access may be purchased for upward of $250 per month. Generally, dial-up access is billed on an hourly basis, while dedicated dial-up access is billed as a flat rate for unlimited connection time.

For dial-up and dedicated modem connections, the connection speeds can range from 2.4 Kbps to 28.8 Kbps. Dedicated 28.8 Kbps dial-up connections may be obtained for approximately $300 a month and usually require a one-time setup fee of approximately $200.

e. Heavy-duty Internet access: Leased lines

Leased lines are the most expensive and most flexible connections to the Internet, and usually only commercial sites that provide 24-hour availability Internet services to a large base of customers will need them.

Leased lines are permanently connected from your business premises to the computer system at your ISP. A leased-line telephone connection cannot be used for regular telephone service: you can't unplug your communications equipment from the telephone jack and plug in a telephone and expect to get a dial tone. A leased line can be used only with specific types of communications equipment.

With a leased line, there is no need to dial up the remote site, as you are always connected, simply because your equipment is connected to the line. The communications method used between you and your ISP is SLIP or PPP (see section below).

Leased lines require a CSU/DSU, a device that converts the leased-line communications signal to a format that may be used by your computer. If more than one computer is using the leased line, another piece of equipment called a router is often added. A router allows multiple computers to talk to each other and to external devices such as the CSU/DSU.

Leased-line connections usually have a higher bandwidth than dial-up connections, and can range in speed from 56 Kbps to 1.544 Mbps and higher. Higher leased-line speeds are available but are usually used only by large corporations.

Costs for 56 Kbps and T1 (access equivalent of 1.544 Mbps) leased-line connections can vary significantly. Users in the United States may purchase T1 connections for as little as $2,500 a month. Users in Canada and Europe can expect to pay higher rates. Leased-line installation and monthly fees may be paid directly by you to the telephone company, or they may be paid indirectly through your ISP, depending on your contractual arrangement. Leased lines have a flat rate; the rate is not usage based.

The equipment you will need will usually be recommended, and possibly even supplied, by your ISP. This equipment is generally not available through local computer supplies stores and must be special ordered from your local telephone company or telecommunications equipment company. You should arrange for your ISP to install and test this equipment at your business site. You should have your ISP show you how to check that equipment is working correctly and how to ensure everything will start up correctly after a power failure.

Table #1 compares the different bandwidths and their costs.

f. Internet access for the masses: Shell accounts, SLIP, and PPP

In the Internet world, the term *account* refers to the service you purchase from an ISP that allows you access. There are various types of accounts available to you. For dial-up connections, you have three further sub-choices of how to access the Internet: a *shell* account, a *SLIP* account, or a *PPP* account.

1. Shell accounts

A shell account allows you to access the Internet using a set of programs running on the ISP's computer. You connect to the ISP's computer using a data communications application such as ProComm, Telix, or CrossTalk.

In general, shell accounts provide text-oriented *interfaces* (the presentation of the information on the computer monitor) and you are not able to view any graphics, sound, or images that otherwise might be available through the Internet services.

Shell accounts are inconsistent between ISPs in terms of function and use. With a shell account, you are limited to using one Internet tool at a time during your on-line activities. While casual users won't be too affected or concerned, the shell

TABLE #1
ACCESS SPEEDS AND TYPICAL COSTS: A COMPARISON

Shared dial-up	**Speed/costs**
Bandwidth	2.4/9.6/14.4/28.8 Kbps
Equipment	$200
Recurring line costs	voice line (~$20)
ISP monthly fee	$20

Dedicated dial-up	**Speed/costs**
Bandwidth	2.4/9.6/14.4/28.8 Kbps
Equipment	$200
Recurring line costs	voice line (~$50)
ISP monthly fee	$300

Dedicated ISDN dial-up	**Speed/costs**
Bandwidth	56 to 128 Kbps
Equipment	$500
Recurring line costs	ISDN BRI line (ISDN rates vary widely; some rates are usage sensitive, others are a flat rate.)
ISP monthly fee	$500

Leased line	**Speed/costs**
Bandwidth	56 Kbps to 1.544 Mbps
Equipment	$500 - $5,000
Recurring line costs	Leased line (~ $400 - $1,000)
ISP monthly fee	$500 - $2,000

Note: Initial setup costs for telephone company and ISP vary in all cases.

account does present a limitation that experienced users will find bridling. Given an option, typical shell accounts are not an attractive choice for Internet access. However, they may be suitable for users with limited Internet service needs, such as e-mail (discussed in the next chapter).

2. SLIP and PPP

SLIP stands for serial line Internet protocol, while PPP stands for point to point protocol. SLIP and PPP are both means by which your computer can talk to the ISP's computer to gain direct access to Internet resources. From the user's point of view, SLIP and PPP provide essentially the same function. The primary difference is that PPP is technically more efficient and flexible. Many ISPs, and all major computer software for PCs, support both SLIP and PPP, and access is often advertised as "SLIP/PPP accounts" to reflect this.

An important benefit of using a SLIP/PPP account is that you interact with Internet services using computer programs resident on your computer. These programs typically have user interfaces consistent with other personal applications on your computer with which you will be familiar. You have a great deal of flexibility in the choice of software that you can use to access Internet services. A further benefit of using a SLIP/PPP account is that computer software currently available for IBM PCs or Macintosh computers allows you to make use of more than one Internet tool at a time — allowing you to squeeze the most out of your connect time.

A potential barrier to using a SLIP/PPP account is that it requires a minimum of a 386 IBM compatible PC and *at least* a 9.6 Kbps dial-up modem connection to be even marginally useful. Based on our experiences, you must have at least a 386, 33 Mhz PC with 4Mb of RAM running Windows and connected to the Internet via a 14.4 Kbps modem for a SLIP/PPP account to be effective.

g. *Next generation dial-up connections: Integrated Services Digital Network (ISDN)*

As an alternative to the typical dial-up modems, a telephone service known as Integrated Services Digital Network (ISDN) is now becoming available. This service allows a customer to establish a high-speed data connection ranging from 56 Kbps to 128 Kbps. ISDN can be used on a dedicated or on-demand dial-up basis, and is a good compromise if you need high access speeds for short periods of time. If ISDN is available in your area and is supported by your ISP, you should consider this as an alternative to 28.8 Kbps modems.

ISDN service varies dramatically in cost and availability. The ISDN rate structure can vary from a fixed monthly fee to a usage-based fee, or a combination of the two. ISDN costs can be as inexpensive as $20 a month to upward of $100 a month, depending on your local telephone company. Moreover, to take advantage of ISDN, you will need a high-end PC (e.g., a 486 PC) and a special data modem. This ISDN-specific modem can cost upward of $300.

3.

A guide to the Internet toolbox

a. What can I do once I'm connected?

Once you are connected to the Internet, you have access to a wide range of computing and information resources, as well as to people and businesses located around the world. Internet tools enable you to —

- gain access to remote computer systems,
- participate in discussion groups,
- search for and retrieve information,
- send and receive e-mail,
- exchange electronic files, and
- find Internet sites through on-line directories.

To "surf the Net," you will need to understand the following:

(a) Internet tools and their capabilities

(b) Internet addresses and uniform resource locators (URLs)

(c) How to find things on the Internet

What kinds of tools exist and what are they used for? Table #2 summarizes the most popular Internet tools. These tools are described in greater detail throughout this chapter. Knowing the names of the tools and what people use them for will be important to you, as you will likely encounter them during the

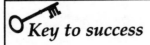

Key to success

Get firsthand knowledge!

Your window into the Internet can vary significantly, depending on the type of software, method of access, and quality of the ISP you use. We strongly recommend that you actually try out the Internet before you make a significant commitment to doing business on it — this is the only way to get the "lay of the land." Throughout the book, we provide the Internet addresses of representative Internet resources that you may want to visit.

Note: While all addresses were valid at the time of printing, the Internet is a dynamic environment and the addresses or associated resources may change over time.

course of your interactions with the Internet community. These tools and others may be purchased at a local computer store or can be obtained for minimal or no charge off the Internet in the form of freeware or shareware. Finding and addressing Internet resources is discussed later in this chapter and in chapter 4.

All of the Internet tools are based on a series of open, nonproprietary standards that anyone is free to use. This means that there are no royalties collected or limitations on the use of the Internet standards: for example, anyone who wants to write an e-mail program may do so, and, if he or she follows the standard exactly, it is reasonable to expect that the resulting program will be able to "talk" to other Internet-connected computers that support the e-mail standards. It is because of these well-defined standards that Internet tools work effectively on a global basis.

b. Are the tools easy to use?

Initially, Internet tools were used only by experienced computer people. But in the last few years, there has been a major emphasis by software tool vendors to make the Internet easy to access and use. This thrust has had the effect of creating a wide variety of point-and-click Internet tools that require no special computer skills to operate. Some of the software vendors have produced new applications that can get the user from unpacking the software package to operating on the Internet in about 15 minutes.

The software applications themselves are intuitive to use for anyone who is already familiar with PC or Macintosh software programs. Many of these new packages allow you to sign up automatically to a national ISP as part of the program's software installation process. Commercial OSPs are often supported by toll-free product helplines, e-mail product support, and documentation such as user manuals dealing with the setup of their special access software and the various on-line services offered, which comes with the software or can be purchased from a local bookstore. OSPs also provide on-line help instructions, similar to the "help" menu available on most computer applications.

It is encouraging that ISPs are actively working to make the Internet easier for their customers to use. Many already provide user support helplines or e-mail support, and a few even provide initial system setup and new-user training. There are also

TABLE #2
POPULAR INTERNET TOOLS AND THEIR FUNCTIONS

Internet Tool	Basic Function
E-mail	Used to send and receive correspondence or files
Automated e-mail lists	Support e-mail based mailing lists for bulk mailing of correspondence or files
Mailbots, autoresponders, and info-servers	Provide automated handling of e-mail messages where automated responses are appropriate
Telnet	Allows users to connect to remote computers anywhere in the world as though they are local to the computer
FTP	Allows the transfer of files between two computers
WAIS	Allows users to search databases using keywords and search criteria, similar to doing searches at a library
Gopher	Allows the user to access Internet sites for information through a hierarchical series of menus
Usenet	Provides a mechanism for large numbers of people to publicly discuss subjects and exchange information
World Wide Web	Allows users to access Internet sites through an integrated text and (optionally) graphic-based presentation of information, using a hypertext interface
Archie	Provides a searchable database of files and directories at publicly accessible FTP sites
Veronica and Jughead	Provides a searchable database of publicly accessible gopher menus

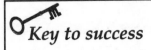
Key to success

Low-cost Internet software!

Freeware is software made available by its creators to anyone who wants it, free of charge, though sometimes restrictions are placed on its use for commercial enterprises. This is in contrast to shareware, where the creator makes software available to anyone who wants it, but expects payment if the user decides to keep the software after an evaluation interval.

Shareware and freeware software is available for all Internet tools and many computer types. The quality of the software varies from poor to very high, matching or even exceeding that of commercially available software.

Shareware and freeware are available on BBSs, at some software shops, and at many file archive sites on the Internet. If you want to save some money, we recommend that you consider what's available.

many publications available to help users make the most of the Internet. The appendix of recommended reading at the back of this book lists some of the ones we consider to be among the most useful.

c. What is an Internet address and uniform resource locator?

Just as a phone number connects you to a person, computer modem, or fax machine, an Internet address connects you to various major Internet tools. Internet addresses may also support connections for custom or proprietary tools. It is important to understand Internet addresses, as they are necessary for you to navigate the Internet.

An Internet address may be expressed as either a series of numbers (e.g., 47.123.456.65), called an *IP address*, or a string of text, separated by periods (e.g., gopher.magmacom.com), called a *domain name*. Either form of Internet address is the electronic equivalent of a telephone number for the host computer (the computer on which an application program is running) and the associated Internet resources or person. For example, when you are running a word processing application on your PC, your PC is the host for the word processing application.

For all Internet tools except e-mail, the address may be written and used in either of the two formats. It is generally not necessary for you to be aware of the semantics of the Internet address itself; it is sufficient to know that Internet tools will accept either format. For instance, "magmacom.com" and "204.191.36.4" are equivalent Internet addresses when provided to most Internet tools.

An Internet address may also have another number appended to it following a colon (e.g., 204.191.36.4:80, magmacom.com:80). The number after the colon is usually referred to as a *port number* and is a refinement that some host computers need, depending on how the applications have been configured by the system administrator.

To reach a person using Internet e-mail, you must identify the recipient along with the domain name format of the Internet address, separated by an "@" character. For instance, to send mail to Brian Hurley, you would send mail to *bhurley@magmacom.com*. The user identification, or "userid," is *bhurley* and *magmacom.com* is the user's ISP's domain name.

Recently, a standard method of specifying Internet addresses called *URL* has become popular. URL is an acronym for uniform resource locator. A URL is the electronic address that is made available to your potential customers to allow them to reach you on the Internet.

URL is a shorthand used to represent both the electronic address and the Internet tool to be used to access resources on the Internet. The basic format of a URL is shown in Figure #1. The URL is accepted as a valid Internet address by World Wide Web tools. How the URL preface may be interpreted is shown in Table #3.

In Figure #1, the "path to file on the host computer" varies, depending on how the computer system and applications are configured on the host computer. This part of the URL may or may not be present and has no use other than to ensure that the Internet tool you are using knows how to access the resource.

Some examples of typical URLs are listed below:

- *mailto:bhurley@magmacom.com*
- *telnet://dragon.achilles.net*
- *gopher://gopher-gw.micro.umn.edu*
- *wais://quake.think.com:210/uumap.src*
- *news:magmacom.announce*
- *http://www.monster.com*
- *ftp://mag1.magmacom.com/~bhurley/ReadMe*

d. E-mail: Fast written communications

The most useful Internet tool is e-mail. E-mail allows you to send a message to one or many recipients with the push of a key. The delivery can be very fast (in seconds or minutes); however, the exact duration for delivery depends on how your ISP's computer is set up and on how many computers are between your ISP's computer and the destination computer.

It costs the same amount of money to send an e-mail message to someone in Russia as it does to send the message across town. More people have access to e-mail on the Internet than any other Internet tool: users in 160 countries access e-mail.

Two terms that you may often encounter in relationship to Internet e-mail are *.sig* or *dot signature*. These terms refer to the

FIGURE #1
ANATOMY OF AN INTERNET UNIFORM RESOURCE LOCATOR (URL)

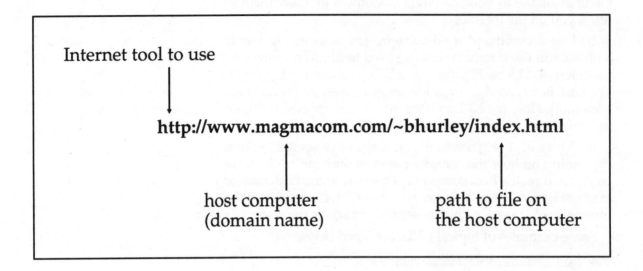

TABLE #3
URL PREFACES

URL preface	Internet tool required to access the resource at the indicated Internet address
gopher://	Gopher application
telnet://	Telnet application
ftp://	File transfer protocol application (FTP)
news:	Usenet newsgroup reader
wais://	Wide area information service (WAIS)
mailto:	Electronic mail
http://	World Wide Web browser application

last few lines of text that are often attached to outgoing e-mail messages. These last few lines are intended to give information on how to reach the sender, and often include a disclaimer when the sender is using a business account for personal reasons (e.g., "these views are my own and do not necessarily represent those of my employer").

Recently, e-mail signatures have also been used to include a very brief advertising blurb. For example, one signature that a businessperson might append to the end of all his or her e-mail correspondence might read:

```
==================================================
John Mills, President      Widget World Inc.

123 Oak Street             "We make the world's BEST Widgets"
Forest, Nevada             For more information, visit us at
PH: 123-567-8910           http://www.widget.com/
FX: 123-567-8911           or send e-mail to info@widget.com


==================================================
```

You may want to use a standard, partial e-mail signature for all business-related correspondence to ensure that a consistent and professional image is presented.

There are large numbers of potential customers who subscribe to large OSPs. A benefit of Internet e-mail is that it may be used to send mail to, and receive mail from, other nonInternet e-mail tools. For example, users on the Internet can send messages to, and receive messages from, the users of OSPs such as CompuServe, America Online, and Prodigy, as well as specialized e-mail services such as MCI Mail.

E-mail messages may be sent to fax machines and pagers, using both informally maintained and commercial e-mail enhancement services, which can lend itself to reduced fax costs, since long distance charges may be avoided. Using e-mail in conjunction with pagers can help keep a salesperson in touch with important messages.

Using e-mail for business correspondence may reduce postage and handling costs for businesses. E-mail can be used in a number of ways, including automated mailing lists and discussion groups

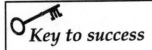

Key to success

Send spreadsheets and word processing files with e-mail!

People tend to think of e-mail as being for text messages only, but you can also attach files for transfer across the Internet using an enhanced e-mail capability called "MIME." The MIME attachment makes it easy to share spreadsheets, presentations, and documents between sites without having to know very much about other Internet tools. MIME is supported by some of the newer e-mail software packages.

For software packages that don't support MIME, files can also be transferred via e-mail using other software programs. In this case, the recipient must go through a decoding process to recreate the files from the e-mail messages he or she receives.

The most common encoding/decoding approach is known as *uuencoding*. However, this method can be tedious and time-consuming.

and as automated information servers. These applications are described below.

E-mail is very flexible. It can be used to access other Internet tools such as Gopher, Archie, the Web, and FTP, albeit in a tedious fashion. However, if you have nothing else but e-mail as your means of accessing the Internet, having an option is always better than not having an option!

1. E-mail cautions

E-mail is not perfect, and all users should be aware of certain things:

(a) *E-mail can be forged.* Any novice user can forge an e-mail message, generating a message that looks like it came from someone else by using existing e-mail programs for PCs connected to the Internet, using a SLIP or PPP connection.

(b) *E-mail can be easily disseminated.* Don't put anything in an e-mail message that you wouldn't want to have disseminated further. E-mail makes it very easy for someone to forward a message to a large number of recipients.

(c) *E-mail is not guaranteed to be delivered.* Similar to traditional mail delivery, mail delivery over the Internet is not guaranteed. Mail can be lost en route because of corruption of the files at the intermediate computer systems where the mail is stored, or because of network or computer congestion along the way to the final destination. If e-mail is lost, the intended recipient or the sender will not receive any indication that there has been a problem. Some Internet mail application programs provide remote confirmation of receipt, which is the electronic equivalent of registered mail — but this is not ubiquitously supported.

We have never had any problems with mail not being delivered, but you should be aware of this possibility. If your mail cannot be successfully delivered, perhaps because the Internet address is incorrect or some problem prevents the intermediate computer from delivering the message to the intended recipient's computer, your outgoing message will be returned to you with a message that it is undeliverable.

(d) *E-mail is not secure.* There is no guarantee that the privacy of your message will be respected as it travels through the Internet to its destination. Your e-mail may be temporarily stored by many different computer systems along the way. At each computer system, and to a lesser degree, on each of the communication links that carry the information, the contents of your e-mail are accessible.

(e) *All e-mail is not created equal!* When an OSP or BBS offers e-mail, do not assume that this service includes connection to the Internet. For instance, until recently, the basic e-mail service provided on CompuServe did not include access to the Internet. Charges were added for each message sent and received from the Internet, based on the size of the message. On BBSs, the same may be true.

There are other significant differences between various e-mail services. For instance, the length of message that may be sent and received may vary. As well, not all e-mail services support Internet e-mail enhancements such as MIME. The timeliness of delivery and receipt of e-mail for the service provider may also vary. For instance, some e-mail providers will forward your message toward its destination immediately upon receipt. Other providers may save messages, sending them on late in the evening.

2. Automated e-mail mailing lists and discussion groups

There are a number of specialized programs available that support e-mail based mailing lists. A mailing list program manages e-mail correspondence among a group of interested people. You may send an e-mail message to a special address or ask to be added to a particular mailing list. Some mailing lists are read-only, dedicated to sending out information from an organization or person to a group of interested people, while other mailing lists offer a forum for discussion among all mailing-list subscribers.

To send messages to a discussion mailing list, you send an e-mail message to a designated mailing-list address. That message is then forwarded to all other mailing-list subscribers. Before being forwarded, the message may be reviewed by a moderator to ensure that the integrity of the mailing list is maintained, and any e-mail not directly relevant to the topic of the mailing list may be filtered out. There are discussion mailing lists and information-only mailing lists on almost every topic imaginable.

Mailing list services may be purchased for as little as $25 per month, with an initial setup fee of $30.

3. Mailbots, autoresponders, and info-servers

There is a class of Internet-related computer applications known variously as *mailbots*, *autoresponders*, and *info-servers*. These automated e-mail applications all have similar functions, their basic purpose being to process, immediately and without human intervention, all received e-mail messages. These applications exist primarily to provide "canned" e-mail messages. For instance, a potential customer wanting more information on a specific product advertised in a magazine could simply send an empty e-mail message to the address *info@company.com*. Shortly afterward, the customer would receive an e-mail message containing significantly more detail than the print advertisement. Canned messages usually provide information on how to contact a salesperson if more information is needed.

For businesses, these applications represent a great opportunity to handle typical questions in a cost-effective and consistent manner. The simple addition of an e-mail address on a print advertisement is a good way to reach more customers. Automated e-mail services such as these can be purchased for upwards of $25 per month, and can respond to customer queries 24 hours a day, seven days a week.

e. Telnet: Remote computer access without long distance charges

Telnet is a powerful Internet tool that lets you connect to a computer that may be in another city or country. The clear benefit that Telnet provides to the user is the freedom to dial up on the Internet to a computer anywhere in the world, without having to worry about long distance charges.

Telnet is the Internet equivalent of the data communication program (text only) that you would use with your modem to dial up a BBS or OSP. The only difference is that Telnet uses the

Internet in place of the telephone network to access another computer.

Clearly, a business set up on the Internet benefits from the removal of the access barrier that long distance charges may present to potential customers. The same holds true when a business wants to access its own computer systems in branches operating in different cities or countries.

Through Telnet, users with SLIP/PPP accounts may connect to multiple remote computers at the same time — using one telephone connection to the ISP. (This is in contrast to normal PC use, where your ability to interact with remote computer systems is limited primarily by the number of telephone lines and modems connected to your computer.) At the same time, a remote computer connected to the Internet with SLIP/PPP that allows remote users to access the computer using Telnet may also support multiple users at once over a single dial-up or leased line connection. Access to computers via Telnet is controlled by a login name and password mechanism.

Telnet is an attractive tool that can extend the reach and effectiveness of a BBS. Telnet offers ready access for businesses wanting to set up customer information services that take advantage of mature bulletin board software packages readily available for PCs.

f. File transfer protocol (FTP): Moving files across the Internet

File transfer protocol, or FTP as it is usually referred to, is a popular Internet tool that allows users to move files between different computer systems. Any files can be transferred using FTP, including spreadsheets, and database or word processing files.

A term you will often hear in conjunction with FTP and the Internet will be "anonymous file archive sites" or "anonymous FTP sites"; the terms are generally used interchangeably and refer to a computer system that supports a collection of useful — and sometimes not so useful — computer data files, text files, or application programs that are available for retrieval by anyone interested. Access to FTP resources on the Internet is controlled by a login name and password mechanism. In the case of anonymous file archive sites, the login name is always "anonymous" and the password can be anything, but is usually the user's e-mail address.

For businesses, FTP provides a proven mechanism to distribute electronic catalogues and computer software, and to transfer general files between computer systems. Many software businesses currently on the Internet make use of FTP to distribute software upgrades.

g. *Wide area information system (WAIS)*

Wide area information system (WAIS) is an Internet tool that allows you to search databases over the Internet using plain English, rather than computer jargon, query commands.

WAIS is a good tool for searching the vast amounts of text-oriented material available on the Internet. Requests to WAIS applications are made by specifying keywords and logical relationships. WAIS databases will respond with a list of resources matching the query in the order of how closely the resource matches the search request. The drawback, particularly for large WAIS databases, is that WAIS can present you with far more information than you want, or than is possible to wade through, if the searching is not done in a well-thought-out manner.

WAIS databases may be accessed using a variety of methods, including Telnet, the Web, and Gopher, and through custom application software (residing on your PC and communicating over a SLIP/PPP account).

For the business user, WAIS provides an information resource. For the business entrepreneur, WAIS represents a tool for making custom information services available.

h. *Gopher: Menu-driven Internet resource navigator and tool integrator*

Gopher provides access to information and data files that may be spread across many different computer systems connected to the Internet. Gopher provides you with a menu (which appears as a list of one-line descriptions or file names) from which to make a choice. Multiple levels of menus help organize the information in the same manner as filing cabinet drawers and folders. Gopher presents Internet resources such as files, Telnet services, WAIS, and other custom applications as other menu items which may be chosen, making accessing information transparent to the user; you simply point and click, without needing any further knowledge of how that particular Internet application works.

To the user, Gopher is a barrier remover. Gopher reduces using the Internet to a simple task of traversing menus until the information is found. To the business user, Gopher provides a pre-built infrastructure on which to offer information to the customer.

i. Usenet newsgroups

Usenet, or NetNews as it is sometimes known, is an electronic bulletin board that supports discussion topics and information distribution. Usenet is a very popular feature of the Internet with over 10,000 discussion groups covering topics ranging from the highly technical to the completely trivial. However, not all discussion groups are available to all users. The main reason for this disparity is that Usenet is informally run, and providing Usenet newsgroups on a particular computer system can consume a great deal of computer resources. Therefore, each computer site administrator determines which newsgroups to carry. Some newsgroups are regional, by state or country, or local, by city or organization.

Usenet newsgroups have cryptic names such as *alt.newusers.announce* or *comp.binaries.pc*. When you access Usenet, you are usually presented with a list of active newsgroups available. You can then select a specific newsgroup and receive a list of e-mail messages that have been posted, or sent, to that newsgroup.

You may view all messages posted to any newsgroup that is carried by your ISP. You may also post a message to any newsgroup. Some newsgroups are moderated, in the same manner as some mailing lists. Newsgroups range from discussion-oriented groups to groups dedicated to the distribution of binary files of PC software, graphic images, or sounds.

Posted articles are distributed among computer sites that exchange news, and are held at each site for a variable amount of time before they expire and are automatically deleted from the site. The amount of time that a posted message is available depends on the computer administrator and is usually based on computer resources. Each newsgroup article that is stored for viewing takes up space on a computer's hard disk, and the many thousands of messages that may arrive each day can quickly exceed several hundred megabytes of disk space per day.

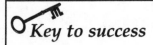

It is important to note that the Usenet is not error free and, consequently, not all messages posted to the newsgroup may be seen at all sites where the newsgroup is being viewed. This leads to Usenet participants often requesting the re-transmission of a message or file. Also, the time at which an article is posted to the time any particular user reads it at any particular site may range from seconds to days. Since articles are passed from computer to computer, as with e-mail, there is no guarantee of timely distribution or of delivery at all. Usenet is an informal network, and you must accept it for what it is.

Even considering its limitations, Usenet offers a powerful tool for business. Taking Usenet at face value, it provides an information resource to the user and businessperson on a wide variety of topics. Through active participation, Usenet can provide businesspeople with the ability to establish contacts with others of similar interests.

j. World Wide Web: Multimedia Internet navigator and viewer

The Web tool (alternatively referred to as WWW, W3, or simply "the Web") is considered by many to be the main reason for the recent explosive interest in the Internet. This tool is based on a concept called *hypertext*. To the user, the Web presents a graphics and text page of information that has pictures or text highlighted to stand out from other text or graphics. Clicking on the highlighted areas will automatically bring the user to a new "page" of information, graphic, sound, or video clip, usually expanding on or related to the highlighted text previously selected. The links can be to a resource residing on a computer anywhere on the Internet. Finding information on the Internet is as simple as reading a book and flipping the pages.

The real attraction of the Web is its ability to integrate multimedia and networking in a seamless manner. However, unless you know what you want, finding information can still be challenging; searching the Web can be the equivalent of flipping through a library of books lying in a jumble on the floor (more information about how to find things on the Web is provided later in chapter 4).

The Web has a lot of jargon associated with it, some of which is useful to know. Programs that allow you to access the Web are referred to generically as *browsers* or *web browsers*. Browsers allow you to request and retrieve Web documents, known as *Web pages* or *home pages*. Computer programs that receive and respond to requests to transfer Web pages are known as *Web sites* or *Web servers*.

Web pages are written in a standard language known as *hypertext markup language*, or HTML as it is more commonly referred to. HTML allows Web-page designers to specify the look and feel of the page. A single business Web site can consist of many individual HTML data files, each representing another page of information that a customer can access using a Web browser. Graphics and images appear in a Web page simply by being referenced in the HTML document: the Web browser reads the HTML reference and accesses the stored graphics file. Graphics and image data are kept in separate files from the text-oriented HTML documents.

A useful feature of HTML documents and some browsers is the ability to create a form that you can fill out. The form can include various types of entry methods, ranging from unconstrained text input to constrained menu choices. After filling out the form, you can send it off with the simple click of a button. HTML documents may also be linked to programs to perform almost any task imaginable. These links to programs are referred to as CGI scripts.

As with any other Internet activity, information that flows between computer sites may be monitored. Some Web browsers, notably the Netscape Navigator, support security features that encode the information being sent between the user and the computer site to ensure that the transaction is confidential. Currently, however, there is no set standard which is supported by all Web browsers and resource sites.

The Web is the most promising Internet tool. Using the Web's most basic capabilities, any number of business applications, most notably advertising and catalogue publishing, are possible with a minimum of effort and cost.

As the HTML standard for the Web continues to evolve, so do the capabilities for the presentation of Web pages. This evolution continues to build the usability of the Web for both general Internet users and business interests.

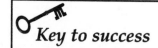

Key to success

Best Web browser
The current leading commercial software package that supports the Web is from Netscape Communications, whose browser software, known commercially as *Netscape Navigator*, is used by a significant number of Internet users. Netscape is available on the Internet as shareware for download to your computer from *http://home.netscape.com/*.

k. Tool evolution

The set of Internet tools available is widely deployed and will define what you can do with the Internet. However, the open nature of the Internet allows anyone to create and distribute new tools that build on top of existing ones, or that stand alone as tools in their own right. As commercialization of the Internet increases, the number and type of tools are expected to develop with increasing velocity, fueled by large commercial interests as well as by entrepreneurs.

l. How do I match Internet tools to business needs?

Like the fax machine or telephone, the Internet is a communications tool for business. The Internet provides opportunities to enhance existing businesses, while at the same time changing their competitive nature and physical operations. The Internet tools may be used to support many different specific business activities involving communication with the customer or communication within the business. At their most basic level, all Internet tools facilitate communication between computers and computer users.

At the most elemental level, business communication may be characterized as follows:

- Public discussion between people (e.g., conference)
- Private person-to-person communication (e.g., business correspondence)
- Public communication to anyone (e.g., advertising)
- Public communication to specific people (e.g., mailing list)
- Communication to electronic devices (e.g., faxing a paper)

The Internet tools can support business communication in any number of ways. Making a decision of which tool is best for your business can be difficult, since often there are many variations on how the tools can be used.

To borrow an old adage, when it comes to deciding which tool is best for your business, use the correct tool for the job. In some cases, there may be more than one tool possible, so the final choice must be balanced against best fit, applicability, and cost. It may sometimes make sense to support multiple tools to cover all the bases, and in fact, it is not uncommon to see businesses on the Internet doing just that!

A business that uses elements of the Web, e-mail, and news-group tools will be able to address the bulk of the Internet users. Applications like Telnet, FTP, and Gopher are used to a lesser extent, but do have potential to enhance your business.

Table #4 shows a breakdown of the use of various Internet tools, and will help you determine the usefulness of the Internet for your specific business needs.

TABLE #4
INTERNET TOOLS AND THEIR BUSINESS POTENTIAL

Business function	E-mail	Telnet	FTP	WWW	Gopher	WAIS	Usenet
Public discussion between interested persons (e.g., conference)	best						good
Private person-to-person (e.g., business correspondence)	best						
Public communication to anyone (e.g., advertising)	good			best	good		good
Public communication to specific persons (e.g., mailing list)	best			good	good		good
Communication to electronic devices (e.g., faxing)	best			good			
Accessing computer services (e.g., information databases)	good	good		good	good	good	
File transfers between computer systems	good		best	good	good	good	

4.

How do I find things on the Internet?

Today, if you want to find the phone number for a local, nonInternet business, you can rely on the newspaper, the Yellow Pages, radio, television, and billboards to find it. However, to get an address for a specific Internet-based business can be difficult, to say the least. For instance, it is difficult to connect to the Internet and pull up a list of all Internet businesses that sell flowers. There are various informally maintained on-line mechanisms, but as experienced users, we don't find them very effective in terms of speed and utility; they certainly do not approach the effectiveness of traditional Yellow Page directories. There *are* Internet directories being published in book form, but, in general, the content is out of date and incomplete in a short period of time.

It is usually difficult to determine a specific person's or business's Internet address. There is no single, definitive repository for Internet resources. This is perhaps one of the biggest impediments to (and ironically, as described in chapter 7, one of the biggest opportunities for) commercial exploitation of the Internet. Chapter 8 discusses methods to gain visibility of your business's Internet address by making the best use of the tools available.

The following sections point you in the right direction if you wish to explore some of the Internet resources or search for potential competition.

a. Internet address domain names

There is a central administrative authority for Internet domain names that maintains an on-line directory. This directory is available using the Telnet and Web tools on the Internet. It is possible to search using a company name or part of a company name. The directory will return the domain name and information about the administrative contact.

It is useful to note that without using a directory service it is possible to guess the domain name for many businesses. For instance, IBM is *ibm.com*, Apple is *apple.com*. If you are looking for associated Web, FTP, or Gopher services for such businesses, you can usually derive the URL by adding "www," "ftp," or "gopher" in front of the domain name (e.g., *http://www.ibm.com/* or *http://www.apple.com/*).

b. E-mail user addresses

There are no comprehensive lists or directories containing e-mail addresses, though work is progressing in the Internet community to provide an on-line solution to address this obvious deficiency. There have been books published that contain some Internet e-mail addresses, but they are not comprehensive or up to date.

c. Listings of on-line mailing lists

There are a tremendous number of mailing lists available on the Internet. However, there is no single comprehensive listing of all available mailing lists. Two of the larger mailing list directories are from Neo Soft and MIT.

d. Lists and databases of Telnet resources

There is no formal directory service for Telnet resources. However, a good place to start looking is the hytelnet, an informally maintained searchable database of publicly accessible Telnet resources on the Internet. The database primarily contains educational and research-oriented resource entries and it is not commercially oriented or comprehensive. Hytelnet directories may be accessed using any Telnet, Web, or Gopher tools. Telnet resources are also listed as resources as part of Gopher and Web informal directories and lists.

Internet domain names directory

Searchable domain name database (Network Solutions Inc.)
telnet://rs.internic.net
http://www.internic.net/

E-mail address directories

Internet address finder (Innovation Insights, Inc.)
http://www.iaf.net/

Commercial service that allows users to register e-mail addresses and free database searches (Four11 On-line User Directory)
http://www.four11.com/

On-line mailing list directories

List of publicly accessible mailing lists (Neo Soft)
http://www.neosoft.com/internet/paml/

List of publicly accessible mailing lists (MIT)
ftp://rtfm.mit.edu/pub/usenet/news.answers/mail/mailing-lists

Telnet directories

Hytelnet information page (Northern Lights Internet Solutions)
http://www.lights.com/hytelnet

List of Telnet accessible resources
gopher://liberty.uc.wlu.edu/11/internet/new_internet/new_hytelnet/

List of Telnet accessible BBSs (SBI - Richard Mark's Select BBSs on the Internet)
http://dkeep.com/sbi.htm

e. Finding public FTP sites and associated files using Archie

An important resource provided by the Internet is the multitude of publicly accessible FTP file archives that provide information and various computer programs. FTP by itself is a great tool when you know what files you want and where they are. There are some informally maintained lists of public FTP sites. However, if you don't know the specific location of the file then you will be in for a long and tedious Internet Easter egg hunt. That is, unless you use Archie.

Archie is an Internet tool that provides a searchable database of anonymous FTP sites and file names. Users can request Archie to perform a search of the directory and file names in its database for a specific match.

For users who know what they are looking for, perhaps a specific shareware program, this tool is extremely useful. For the business user, this tool provides a useful method for potential customers to find the location of information that you want them to have, for example, electronic catalogues.

Archie databases are informally maintained by various system administrators. Archie is generally accessed using the Telnet tool. It can also be accessed using e-mail, along with some Gopher and Web tools, which may provide easy interfaces or links to Archie servers.

Despite its potential usefulness, Archie search requests can take a long time to complete, partially because of the popularity of the service. Moreover, the resulting volume of information may be overwhelming and take time to wade through. However, when compared with the time you would have to take to find a particular file by visiting different anonymous FTP sites, Archie is a real timesaver.

f. Searching gopherspace: Jughead and Veronica

As with public FTP sites, there are both informal lists and search tools to help the user find information distributed in various Gopher sites. Two specific search tools are available: Jughead and Veronica. Jughead and Veronica are similar except in the degree of information contained in their databases, Veronica being more exhaustive.

FTP directories

Exhaustive list of public archive FTP sites (NCSA)
http://hoohoo.ncsa.uiuc.edu/ftp/intro.html

Archie (NCSA)
http://hoohoo.ncsa.uiuc.edu/archie.html

Gopher directories

List of Veronica servers
*http://www.yahoo.com/yahoo/
Computers/Internet/Veronica/*

List of Jughead servers
*gopher://honor.uc.wlu.edu:70/11/
gophers/jugheads*

Veronica (University of Koeln)
gopher://veronica.uni-koeln.de:2347/7

Veronica (University of Texas)
gopher://veronica.utdallas.edu:2348/7

Veronica (University of Manitoba)
gopher://gopher.umanitoba.ca:2347/7

Veronica (PSINet)
gopher://info.psi.net:2347/7

Veronica (SUNET)
gopher://veronica.sunet.se:2347/7

Veronica (NYSERNet)
gopher://empire.nysernet.org:2347/7

Usenet starting points

Usenet newsgroup listings and
associated FAQs (MIT University)
ftp://rtfm.mit.edu/pub/

List of Usenet FAQs
(Ohio State University)
*http://www.cis.ohio-state.edu/
hypertext/faq/usenet/FAQ-List.html*

Veronica is a tool that provides a searchable database of Gopher menus and is generally accessed using the Gopher tool, but can also be accessed using Telnet, e-mail, and Web tools. Veronica may be thought of as the equivalent of a phone directory for Gopher servers. If you are looking for a specific resource on the Internet but don't know where to start looking, Veronica can be a real timesaver. The only drawback is that connecting to a Veronica application can be difficult, since many of the servers are provided informally by educational institutions and are heavily used by the Internet community.

g. *Plumbing the depths of Usenet*

Usenet consists of many newsgroups, all of which may or may not be available from a particular ISP. The best way to determine which newsgroups are available from your ISP is to start up your Usenet tool. It will automatically retrieve all newsgroups that are available from your ISP and give you the option of selecting which ones you wish to browse or participate in.

Once connected to the Internet, it is also possible to use the FTP tool to retrieve a master list of active newsgroups from an archive maintained at MIT. If you want access to a newsgroup that is not available from your ISP, ask your ISP if it can obtain a newsfeed for that particular newsgroup. You will likely find that it will try to accommodate your request.

Most newsgroups have FAQs which describe the intent of the newsgroup and guidelines for participants. Finding FAQs is quite straightforward, as there are well-established sources on the Internet where they are archived. If you want to use only the Usenet tool, you can obtain relevant FAQs by monitoring the appropriate newsgroup for a week or two: the FAQ will eventually be posted by the author.

Another surefire approach is to monitor the newsgroup *news.answers*, as all FAQs are eventually posted here. FAQs are also accessible using FTP and Web tools at the locations given in the sidebar.

If you want to search Usenet newsgroup articles without monitoring newsgroups on a continuous basis, you can take advantage of an on-line service such as DejaNews. DejaNews is a Web-based service that allows you to search a large archive of newsgroup articles using keywords. DejaNews maintains a historical database of all posted articles for a month for most newsgroups, and for an entire year for selected newsgroups. If you are looking for postings that deal with a specific topic, this service is invaluable. InfoSeek also provides a similar pay-per-use service.

DejaNews
http://www.dejanews.com/

InfoSeek
http://www.infoseek.com/

h. Finding WAIS databases

There is no formal directory service for WAIS databases on the Internet. However, the company that sells WAIS software does offer an informal, yet very extensive, directory of publicly accessible WAIS databases. This is a very good place to start your search.

Since WAIS databases can be accessed using the Telnet, Gopher, and World Wide Web tools, you will also be able to search for them using the informal directory services associated with those other tools.

WAIS directories

List of all known publicly accessible WAIS databases in the world (WAIS Inc.)
http://wais.wais.com:80/wais-dbs/

List of WAIS databases (Yahoo)
http://www.yahoo.com/Computers/ World_Wide_Web/Databases_and_ Searching/WAIS

i. Unweaving the World Wide Web

The Web does not provide any formal directory service but, instead, relies primarily on a number of informal directories made available by educational and business institutions as a courtesy to the Internet community. Additions to and searches of most directories are free of charge.

A relatively recent phenomenon has been the formation of some pay-per-use Internet resource directories such as InfoSeek. The growth of these directories is to the benefit of businesses wanting to use the Internet as a resource for information researching, since the pay-per-use databases are more comprehensive in content than some of the more popular free databases.

Comprehensive Web directories

Yahoo
http://www.yahoo.com/

WebCrawler
http://www.webcrawler.com/

EINet Galaxy
http://galaxy.einet.net/galaxy.html

Lycos
http://www.lycos.com/

5.

Analyzing your business for its Internet potential

Developing a customized Internet business plan that suits your specific enterprise requires an honest assessment of whether or not your business would benefit from setting up shop in this electronic environment. It is easy to get caught up in the technology and media hype, but ultimately you need to determine whether or not putting your business on-line will result in a net benefit.

So far, we have examined the Internet in terms of its user characteristics and demographics, and the underlying technology and tools available in this new environment. You must now use this knowledge to assess whether the Internet environment is matched to your business objectives and if there is a real fit and opportunity.

You also need to consider that the Internet is a dynamic business environment which is changing almost daily, and that a good business plan should incorporate an understanding of where the Internet is today and where it is going tomorrow. This information can be used as part of your own analysis and will help you examine your business needs against the many business opportunities presented in chapters 6 and 7.

A good Internet business analysis should consist of the seven steps summarized in Figure #2.

FIGURE #2
SEVEN-STEP INTERNET BUSINESS ANALYSIS

1	**Analyze your product or service**	Analyze the product or service that you sell or plan to sell to determine if it is a natural fit to the Internet environment.
2	**Identify your customers**	Determine whether there is a match between your target customers and what the users want.
3	**Establish your business objectives**	Determine what your business objectives on the Internet are (e.g., Do you see it as a long-term or short-term business direction?).
4	**Establish financial commitment**	Determine how much investment you want to make in an Internet presence and the length of time you want to maintain it.
5	**Understand legal issues**	Obtain a general understanding of potential legal issues you may face operating on the Internet, and decide whether you are prepared to take these into account when operating an Internet business.
6	**Understand security issues**	Obtain a general understanding of security-related issues and determine whether you are prepared to invest the necessary resources.
7	**Create a business model and strategy**	Determine your specific business model based on the analysis from steps 1 to 6.

a. Analyzing your product or service

Some products and services have a more natural fit to the Internet than others. If your product or service is information based or electronic in nature, perhaps a time-dependent service such as near real-time stock market information or a software product, it will have a greater range of sales and marketing potential, allowing you to both advertise and sell directly over the Internet. If you are selling products such as clothing or automobiles, the Internet will provide an advertising mechanism, but your products must be provided to the customer by traditional shipping methods.

Take a few minutes to review Tables #5 and #6. They will help you determine the characteristics of your product or service. The last column in each table indicates the relative potential of each of the areas outlined relative to the Internet business environment.

b. Identifying your customers

What type of customer would you like to reach on the Internet? Take a few minutes to think about who your current customers are and what type of customer you would like to reach on the Internet with your existing or new product or service. Review the "Potential" column of Table #5, as it will give you a sense of how effective the Internet might be for your business.

c. Establishing your business objectives

When considering whether you should use the Internet as part of your business, there are a number of questions you should consider, including the following:

(a) What do you envision using the Internet for in your business? Do you see it as an improvement to your business communications environment, an adjunct to your advertising and marketing strategy, or part of an on-line sales effort?

(b) What kind of information or corporate presence do you want to present to the outside world? Do you want a flashy multimedia presentation or a simple e-mail address?

(c) Do you want to be able to survey your customers and be in regular communication with them?

(d) Do you see the Internet as a means to provide on-line customer support?

(e) Do you want to sell and ship products electronically over the Internet?

(f) Would you be worried about competitors reading information on your Internet presence?

(g) Do you envision setting up an Internet presence yourself or hiring a third-party consultant? Do you have the technical skills to run your own Internet presence?

(h) What kind of Internet tools would be the most useful to you — the Web, e-mail, Gopher, or others?

The conclusions you come to by answering these questions can provide additional information to feed into your Internet business plan.

TABLE #5
INTERNET POTENTIAL FOR YOUR PRODUCT OR SERVICE

Business Questions	Description	Potential (H=high; M=medium; L=low)
In what business sector is your current product or service?	Computers and communication	H
	Government and administration	H
	Retail and wholesale industry	H/M
	Manufacturing	L
	Health care	H/M
	Educational services	H
	Financial services	H
	Transportation services	M/L
	Engineering and technical services	M
	Electronic media and entertainment	H
	Construction services	L
	Legal services	M/L
	Consulting and professional services	H
	Hotel and travel industry	H
	Nonprofit organization	H
Is your product a recognizable brand name?	Yes	H
	No	M/L

TABLE #5 — Continued

Business Questions	Description	Potential (H=high; M=medium; L=low)
Is your product or service information based?	Is your information time dependent (i.e., if your customer hears the information tomorrow rather than today, will it make a difference)?	H
	Is your information provided as a service to the community?	H
	Is your information provided to let your customer base know of your company and products?	H
Does your product or service require regular communication with your customer?	Single, one-time transaction	M
	Multiple, repeat transactions	H
	Continuous communications	H
How much does your product or service cost the customer?	High investment for customer	M/L
	Medium investment for customer	H/M
	Low investment for customer	H
Do you sell high or low volumes of your product or service?	High	H
	Medium	H
	Low	H
Is your product or service a commodity item?	Yes	L
	No (Specialty)	H
Is your product or service local, regional, national, or global in nature?	Local	H
	Regional	H
	National	H
	Global	H

TABLE #6
INTERNET POTENTIAL FOR YOUR TARGET MARKET

Business Questions	Description	Potential (H=high; M=medium; L=low)
Are you targeting males or females?	Male	H
	Female	M
What is the typical age range of your customers?	1-10	L
	11-15	L
	16-20	M
	21-30	H
	31-40	H
	41-50	H
	50+	H
Are you selling your product or service in North America or globally?	United States and Canada	H
	Mexico	M
	South and Central America	M/L
	Europe	H
	Far East	M/L
What occupational group are you targeting?	Computer related	H
	Education related	H
	Professional	H
	Management	M
	Other	M/L
What educational backgrounds do your customers have?	High school	M/L
	College	H
	Undergraduate	H
	Masters	H
	Ph.D.	M

TABLE #6 — Continued

Business Questions	Description	Potential (H=high; M=medium; L=low)
In what salary range are your customers?	$ 0 - $ 25,000	L
	25,000 - 50,000	M/H
	50,000 - 75,000	H
	75,000 - 100,000	H
	100,000+	H
What is your typical customer's marital status?	Married	H
	Single	H

d. Determining financial commitment

How much do you want to spend on the Internet component of your business? Today, most smaller businesses are taking a do-it-yourself approach because they want to gain Internet experience as well as keep costs down. Many of the larger companies are hiring professionals because that is more efficient for them. Most businesses' Internet presences are based on Web or e-mail, since these two tools prove to be of greatest use for most operations. Costs of establishing and maintaining your Internet presence vary depending on its sophistication.

If you are a small company or a real do-it-yourselfer, you may want to create your own Internet presence to keep costs down. In these cases, $500 to $1,000 per year can put you on the Internet map with a combination of good quality Web pages and e-mail presence.

If you are a larger company and time is a bigger consideration than money, hiring an Internet consulting firm to create your corporate Web pages may be the most efficient route. Prices from $15,000 to $150,000 are currently being quoted by some consulting firms.

Given the wide range of costs, it is worthwhile shopping around or considering building expertise within your organization in order to minimize unnecessary expense. If your company has many internal departments, a budget for creating an Internet presence may come out of sales, marketing, product management, corporate communications, or the product support department, depending on which department has the greatest need. It is wise to keep the activity within one department to ensure proper coordination within the company and to ensure that money isn't being spent twice between departments.

e. Understanding legal issues

What kinds of legal issues are related to the Internet and on-line technology in general? If you plan to operate your own Internet site or lease space, you must be aware of your legal responsibilities for what you put on the system and how others use it, as well as the changing nature of law surrounding this unique environment. This section will give you a brief overview of things to watch out for.

If you are seriously considering starting up an Internet business and you feel that legal issues may arise because of the nature of your product or service, you should contact a lawyer who specializes in on-line law. Be sure to verify that the lawyer does have actual experience and past clients in this area; many do not since it is such a new and dynamic area. The material provided below is not a substitute for real legal counsel and serves only as a guide to your business planning.

The broad areas of legal consideration include the following:

(a) Commercial tax, contract law, and acceptable use policies

(b) Copyright and use of Internet-available materials

(c) Freedom of speech, censorship, and right to privacy

(d) Criminal law and pornography

Even though the Internet is global, it appears as though U.S. law is being applied as the *de facto* standard to which all users and operators on the network comply. There is no guarantee that this will be the case in coming years, and situations have already arisen where laws foreign to U.S. law have had an impact on service provider and user activity.

If you are targeting a country other than the United States, you should become intimately familiar with its specific laws and you probably should retain a lawyer who practices in the country.

1. Commercial tax, contract law, and acceptable use policies

Performing a global sales transaction over the Internet is the electronic equivalent of performing a mail order transaction. In the mail order business, purchases are made by customers around the world. Commercial tax laws that apply to the mail order business also apply to the Internet business: it is almost a one-for-one business analogy. As with any business, Internet businesses are subject to tax audits and must produce records of transactions to verify taxable income and expenses qualifying for deductions. For most businesses, commercial tax law is straightforward. Other businesses, such as Internet gambling, are attempting to get around paying taxes by capitalizing on the global nature of the Internet community, as well as setting up shop in different tax havens around the world.

When considering setting up your Internet business or presence, you should be very aware of contract law and acceptable use policies, particularly in the following scenarios:

(a) You are directly operating an Internet service for a group of customers on your own Internet service platform.

(b) You are operating your business through a third-party service provider's platform.

(c) You are a service/content provider providing services to a third-party service provider (e.g., you are operating a financial news service and you sell your information to all ISPs for a fee).

(a) Direct service operator

If you are operating a service on the Internet, it is imperative that you understand the rules of conduct and the users' expectations of what your service is providing. Your subscribers need to understand their obligations, rights, and privileges when dealing with your business. Generally, operators of on-line services have their subscribers sign a contractual agreement that covers their financial obligations,

---

Internet gambling confounds tax laws

In the October 1995 issue of *Wired* magazine, an article appeared on Internet gambling issues that discussed how some operators avoided paying U.S. taxes. Currently, legal gambling in the United States is in the order of $500 billion a year.

Some operators have been setting up Internet gambling shops in Caribbean countries such as Turks and Caicos, St. Marten, and Nassau, where tax laws are lax. Internet users can place bets over the Internet and the operators rake in profits without, apparently, being subject to U.S. tax law. Running such an operation is not without risk. The U.S. Interstate Wire Act forbids gambling over a network where the transaction crosses state or international boundaries. Operators entering the United States are subject to having their assets seized by U.S. law enforcement agencies.

permits the service operator to make inquiries about the subscribers' credit worthiness, specifies the service operator's limitation of liability and indemnity with respect to the users' misuse of the computing resources, and spells out the terms and conditions of the service.

This contract provides protection to both parties and creates a uniform environment for all subscribers to your service. Service operators also generally reserve the right to change the content of the service agreement at will (within reason, so as not to scare off their hard-earned subscriber base), as well as reserving the right to monitor users' private messages if there is any suspicious user activity. Service operators may also remove users or their messages and files from the system if the users are not operating under the service provider's acceptable use policies. Forced removal of users is not common, but it does occur.

(b) Operating your business through a third-party service provider

If you are operating your business through a third party, you are considered a user on the service provider's computer and subject to the contractual agreements already described above. However, since you are operating your business through the service provider's system, you may request a clause in the agreement to specify performance of the service. For example, if the operator's system is out of service or busy all the time, this may cost you lost sales and affect your revenue. A contractual clause might state that you expect a specified level of *uptime* or tolerable *downtime* to ensure that your presence on the Internet is not a source of frustration to your potential customers.

You also have a standard business contract relationship between your company and the Internet user wishing to purchase a product or service on-line from your company. You should use a standard purchase agreement for the goods you provide. If you plan to support on-line purchases that are electronically transmitted over the Internet without the use of secure communications, you could be asking for trouble. As a merchant on the Internet, you need to be aware of your financial liability in the case of disputed or fraudulent transactions.

(c) Selling services to a third-party reseller

If you are a service provider who is providing to, or receiving services from, a third-party reseller, both you and the third-party reseller have entered into a contractual agreement to support a service interface with the goal of making money. For example, suppose your new business was serving as a broker for financial information services from different companies. You would receive payment from the various financial service organizations to support their services on your computing facilities, and you might receive a percentage of sales of the various financial services.

Clearly, a financial and contractual agreement exists between your "brokering" business and the various financial service companies working through you. Each of the contracts you negotiate with the other companies would include standard service provider agreements and might also include additional service performance, security, privacy, revenue-sharing, and data ownership clauses.

2. Copyright and use of Internet-available materials

People and companies copyright material because it represents *intellectual property* with the potential for financial return. There is a popular misconception that the Internet is a brave new world where no one need worry about "outdated views" of copyright and where no one owns anything in cyberspace. This view is dead wrong and you could be liable if you violate or infringe someone else's copyright.

Copyright law as it exists today is fairly specific on who owns the intellectual property rights of a specific creation. To give perspective to this concept, current U.S. law states that each person or business owns the copyright to information or a product as soon as it is created, regardless of whether or not "Copyright 1996 Brian Hurley," for example, is written on the information or product, or whether the material was ever formally registered. Naturally, it is best to register your creation at the federal copyright agency, as well as to write the copyright statement on the material, as these precautions will help you if you are ever faced with a court challenge.

So who owns what on the Internet? On the basis of existing copyright law, the creator of the material retains the rights to the material, unless the copyright has been sold by the owner. Also, material generated by employees is often considered to be copyrighted by the employer. To give you an idea of how the laws work, a few examples are provided below:

- Users operating on a service provider's computer system and generating e-mail own the content of the e-mail.

- Users contributing to discussion groups own the content of their contribution to that discussion group.

- Users generating information on behalf of their company do not own the material — their employer does, unless the employee did not sign over his or her copyright ownership to the employer.

On-line copyright information

U.S. Copyright Office, Library of Congress.
gopher://marvel.loc.gov/11/copyright
http://lcweb.loc.gov/copyright

What about freeware and shareware software? Just because there is free software readily available does not mean that the original owners have given up rights to the material. Freeware owners retain the copyright to their material even if they don't want it. Shareware creators not only own the copyright but they also require any long-term user to pay for the use of this software. As well, public domain software generally falls under the same category as freeware in that the original creators own the copyright to the software. If you plan to incorporate any of the free software into your product, service, or business, you should pay attention to issues related to copyright infringement.

What happens when you copy digitized pictures, music, or sound or text files to your system? Again, the original owner or producer of this material still owns the content and you should be careful about how you use this material.

If you are a system operator and support other businesses on your system, ensure that you have a clause in your operator-to-user contract that covers confidentiality of business information to protect yourself in case of a lawsuit. You should be extra careful not to inadvertently disclose any of your users' information in public, lest you be open to litigation. Also, if you are maintaining a database that you created for a business, you, as a system operator, might have ownership of the structure of the database but not the actual data contents.

3. Freedom of speech, censorship, and right to privacy

Freedom of speech, censorship, and the right to privacy — these words are an unending tape that keeps playing again and again because it is the fabric that underlies a free society. What are your responsibilities as a service operator or business in this area? What are your responsibilities as a user on the system? What kind of policies should you set for your employees if they are conducting business over the Internet under

On-line civil liberties information

Electronic Frontier Foundation
http://www.eff.org

your company's banner? These questions are not easy to deal with, and common sense needs to prevail in establishing guidelines for your company in these areas.

The Electronic Communications Privacy Act (ECPA) is the major piece of U.S. federal legislation that deals with the privacy of users engaged in on-line activity. The balance that you need to achieve with your users if you are a system operator is one between their comfort level as subscribers and your need to monitor for criminal or unlawful activity on your system.

The ECPA states that users are not automatically given protection from monitoring of e-mail, data, or program files on a service provider's system. It is imperative that in the system operator-to-user contract, an agreement is reached concerning the level of privacy that will be assured by the operator, as well as a statement of conditions under which the operator can intercept and read the user's private information.

Under the law, system operators have the right to view the information themselves but not to show it to anyone outside their organization (excluding law enforcement officials under certain circumstances). Law enforcement officials must produce search warrants and appropriate documentation in order to seize users' messages if they are conducting an investigation.

Freedom of speech is not necessarily guaranteed if the user is operating outside of the agreements reached in the user-to-system operator contract. If you are operating the system, you will need to specify that you have the right to remove the user and any material that is defamatory, a potential cause of legal liability for the system operator for copyright or criminal reasons, or if the user is engaging in criminal activity.

4. Criminal law and pornography

There is a murky world on the Internet of sexually explicit material that violates various cultural standards and computer law. This is a fringe world that is best avoided if you don't want to land yourself in hot water. Unfortunately, this activity is also currently a fact of life, and it is better to have a strategy for dealing with it before it affects your business adversely.

The major U.S. federal law covering computer crime is the Computer Fraud and Abuse Act (CFAA), which covers situations where there are attacks against a particular installation when hackers trespass, where there is theft of data, or where users on the system exceed their privileges and enter unauthorized parts of the system.

If you are operating a service on the network and you have customers who are conducting illegal activity on your system, law enforcement agencies may shut down your system as a byproduct of their investigation and legal action against one of your users. Even though you haven't done anything wrong, your business may be disrupted or ruined in the process.

Be aware of the laws that relate to crime committed from your system over the rest of the Internet, and always be on guard for the following:

(a) Users on your system operating in questionable legal territory (such as dealing in pornographic material)

(b) Users on your system engaging in activities that promote criminal activity (such as supporting discussion groups on making bombs or breaking into computers)

(c) Users or system operators who promote infringement of copyrighted material

Also be aware that people within the system operator's organization may be involved in such criminal activities without your knowledge.

Any of these situations have the potential to expose you to legal action or repercussions of legal actions. If you are aware of any of these types of activities going on in your system, you must take immediate action to notify the authorities. Do it quickly in order to legally distance yourself, as well as to initiate a proper investigation.

In order to protect yourself against such activities, it is a wise precaution to make users aware in your Internet service contract that you have the right to monitor all their private correspondence, discussion materials, and files. While this presses on the user's right to privacy, it is a necessary precaution to avoid and discourage crime on your system.

If you suspect anything illegal on your system, it is best to contact a qualified lawyer to help protect yourself quickly. A proper security plan should also help protect you to a great extent from potentially difficult situations before they get out of hand.

Key to success

Internet rule of thumb

It is easy to remove confusion about legal implications. Simply remember that anything you have liability for in the nonInternet world, you will also have liability for in the Internet world. Generally, rulings and principles of law normally applied to individuals and corporations are brought over to the Internet environment virtually unchanged.

f. Understanding security issues

One of the biggest issues facing the Internet, and any computer network for that matter, is security. There are three main areas of security relevant to the Internet business:

(a) Fraudulent use of credit card information related to on-line financial transactions

(b) General site and computer security

(c) Informational security

(Also see chapter 8 for more details on different methods of on-line ordering that keep security in mind.)

1. Fraudulent use of credit card information

One of the biggest concerns of businesses doing financial transactions on the Internet is how to conduct secure on-line transactions. Commerce on the Internet consists mainly of passing credit card numbers and expiry date information electronically between the merchant and the customer. To date, however, credit card companies and merchants report that fraud and abuse of credit card information has not been a major problem. This type of financial transaction on the Internet is similar to the current mail order telephone order (MOTO) transaction that occurs when you order tickets or books by phone or mail. There is no face-to-face transaction between the merchant and the customer, and no customer signature is on file.

If you intend to conduct electronic transactions over the network, you should be aware that you are ultimately liable for all charges that are disputed by customers or incurred due to fraud. Established policy based on the contract relationship between the credit card company and the merchant engaged in the purchase will kick in. Because the transaction was not face to face and there is no customer signature on file, the credit card companies have the *right of charge back*, which means that all outstanding charges will end up in the lap of the merchant involved.

Meanwhile, the credit card industry is working feverishly to develop secure transaction encryption technology for greater security when passing credit card number and expiry date information, and possibly also secure personal identification numbers.

One interesting development in the search to make financial transactions more secure is the idea of a third-party certification mechanism for both buyers and sellers of goods over the Internet. CommerceNet, an organization composed of companies mandated to develop business over the Internet, has been running an exploratory program that involves certification of both the purchaser and the vendor. Like traditional credit card companies that pre-certify both parties prior to the transaction, usually through a credit application process, CommerceNet generates an electronic certificate based on public key encryption technology. The certificate is issued by the third-party clearing house (CommerceNet in this case) and is used for authentication by both the buyer and the seller in any given transaction. Computers on either end of the transaction may process the certificate and cause the transaction to complete or to abort.

2. General site and computer security

If you are considering operating your own Internet site, you should be aware of general site and computer security issues. If you are not considering your own operation, you should be aware of them when you deal with a third-party ISP.

There have been a number of books written and movies filmed about unauthorized users breaking into computer systems and stealing information, collecting users' passwords and IDs, as well as classified information. Certainly one of the most famous cases is that of American Kevin Mitnick, a computer hacker arrested by the FBI for stealing over one million dollars in data and over 20,000 credit card numbers. The media often portray with glamor the image of the lone "good guy" computer hacker breaking into someone's computer and saving the free world from some kind of evil aggression. As with all crime, it quickly and forever loses its glamour when the so-called "good guy" comes to visit your computer.

As a system operator or user operating on a system, it is your responsibility to create and follow guidelines to allow for a secure computer system and environment for both you and your customers. The question that arises is, "Where do I start?" Fortunately, there are already some documents published on this subject that you can use as you develop a security policy of your own. These documents are referred to as *Request for Comments* (RFC), and they are freely available at *ftp://nic.ddn.mil*

Recommended books on Internet security

The Computer Privacy Handbook, by Andre Bacard. Berkeley, CA: Peachpit Press, 1995

Firewalls and Internet Security: Repelling the Wily Hacker, by William R. Cheswick and Steven M: Bellovin. Reading, MA: Addison-Wesley, 1994

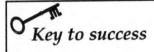

Key to success

Protect your company's computers with firewalls

A combination of hardware and software, a firewall allows only specific individuals, locations, or Internet tools to access your computer or computer network connected to the Internet. A firewall may also be used to prevent external accesses to the Internet from a business's computer system.

If you plan to connect directly to the Internet, you must have a firewall in place or you place your equipment and data at considerable risk. A firewall usually requires technical experience to set up and manage, and is not something that we recommend an Internet business take on itself. Make sure that you understand the risks and have suitably skilled people connect your network to the Internet. A commercial-grade firewall may cost in excess of $25,000. You can obtain more information about firewalls and security at *http://www.tis.com/Home/ Network/Security/Firewalls.*

(RFC 1281 *Guidelines for the Secure Operation of the Internet* and RFC 1244 *Site Security Handbook*).

In *Guidelines for the Secure Operation of the Internet,* six broad guidelines are expanded on, outlining the roles and responsibilities of both the system operator and the users of the system. These general guidelines, quoted from RFC 1281*, are as follows:

(a) Users are individually responsible for understanding and respecting the security policies of the systems (computers and networks) they are using. Users are individually accountable for their own behavior.

(b) Users have the responsibility to employ available security mechanisms and procedures for protecting their own data. They also have a responsibility for assisting in the protection of the systems they use.

(c) Computer and network service providers are responsible for maintaining the security of the systems they operate. They are further responsible for notifying users of their security policies and any changes to these policies.

(d) Vendors and system developers are responsible for providing systems which are sound and which embody adequate security controls.

(e) Users, service providers, and hardware and software vendors are responsible for cooperating to provide security.

(f) Technical improvements in Internet security protocols should be sought on a continuing basis. At the same time, personnel developing new protocols, hardware, and software for the Internet are expected to include security considerations as part of the design and development process.

The RFC expands in greater detail on these themes and provides insight into what these broad objectives mean.

General site and computer security information found in RFC 1244 *Site Security Handbook* ** is relevant to any computer network and provides an outline for a document that could form the basis of your own security policy documents. RFC 1244 provides information on the following:

---

* *Guidelines for the Secure Operation of the Internet,* RFC 1281, by Richard D. Pethia, Stephen D. Crocker, and Barbara Y. Fraser. Released in November 1991.
** *Site Security Handbook,* RFC 1244, by J. Paul Holbrook and Joyce K. Reynolds. Released in July 1991.

(a) Establishing your own official site policy on computer security, including risk assessment, policy interpretation, and documentation

(b) Establishing your own procedures on preventing security problems, including problem detection, recovery, and prevention

(c) Defining multiple strategies for security, including system, account, password, and configuration management

(d) Establishing incident handling procedures that allow you to focus on the problem and not the process

(e) Establishing post-incident procedures, including learning from past incidents, removing vulnerabilities, and adapting your policies and procedures to improve your security system

(f) Familiarizing yourself with computer law, ethics, and general security measures in the industry today

These points will provide you with a good beginning to develop your policy. Some of the policy you set should also be included in your contractual agreements with other companies and users of your service.

3. Informational security

E-mail and file transfer transactions can be viewed, monitored, or intercepted by third parties. One method to combat this personal intrusion is *Pretty Good Privacy* (PGP). PGP is a tool that uses a secure, industry standard encryption technique. (The methods used to perform the encryption are beyond the scope of this book, but see the appendix for a list of further reading materials if you are interested in finding out more about encryption.)

Using a PGP computer program (available as commercial or shareware software), it is possible to encrypt e-mail or files and send them to another person without risk of interception. A useful feature of PGP is that for people to send you encrypted e-mail, they need know only your *public key.* Anyone may send you encrypted mail using your public key as input to the encryption algorithm. However, only you are actually able to decode the message. A business may post its public key and eliminate the need for coordination between the sender and

PGP commercial software vendor
Via Crypt
http://www.viacrypt.com/

receiver by methods other than e-mail to ensure that the encryption keys are known by both parties.

PGP also provides the ability to add a *digital signature* to e-mail messages or files, that leaves the body of the message readable by anyone. The value of the digital signature is that it allows anyone reading the message to confirm that the message actually originated from you and wasn't modified or forged before arriving at its destination.

If you plan to use PGP for your e-mail business correspondence, we recommend that you make your public key readily available by any one of the following methods:

(a) Printing it on the back of your business card

(b) Incorporating it into your e-mail signature

(c) Printing it in your advertised literature

(d) Making it part of an automated e-mail information server

g. *Creating your business model and strategy*

There is much to consider in any business endeavor and an Internet business is no exception. If you have determined from working your way through this chapter that there is indeed an opportunity for your company or organization on the Internet, then you should start putting together your detailed business plan in earnest.

A typical Internet business plan that you could use to approach a bank or group of investors should, at the minimum, contain the following elements:

(a) **Introduction:** This section should outline information about your company, including key personnel, your company's background and market areas, financial data, and a summary of the proposed use of the business loan or financing sought.

(b) **Business plan executive summary:** A concise description of your total plan, outlining key financial and business objectives and risks that are of interest to your potential investors. The Internet business service you plan to offer should be highlighted, along with examples of successful Internet businesses already operating in this area (if any exist).

(c) **Internet and general business goals:** An outline of the financial business goals for your Internet venture, including anticipated revenue projections, market capture, and major business milestones.

(d) **Internet business venture description:** An outline of exactly what Internet-based product or service you plan to offer on the Internet and a statement of how you intend to bring about your business vision.

(e) **Marketing and sales plan:** An outline of how you plan to promote your business and obtain the bottom-line goals outlined earlier. This should include sales forecasts by quarter and sales assumptions about the marketplace, as well as a two- to five-year outlook.

(f) **Operations costs:** A tabulation of expected costs of doing business for the first year, balanced against revenues needed for your business to be profitable.

(g) **Financial forecasts:** Information on your balance sheets, income and expense forecast, cash flow forecast and assumptions, and a break-even analysis.

(h) **Finance, capitalization, and operation loan details:** Information about the loan required to ensure that your Internet-based business gets off on the right foot.

This chapter has provided information to help you determine whether the Internet is the right fit for any of your business ideas, as well as advice on what to look out for in terms of legal and security issues in running your business. You should keep these planning issues in the forefront of your mind as you delve into the myriad of business opportunities presented in chapters 6 and 7.

6.

Enhancing your existing business

What kind of business do you want to do, or can you do, on the Internet? How can the Internet be used to enhance the operation and competitiveness of your business? The answer to these questions depends on many factors, including whether your business objective is to enhance your existing enterprise by using the Internet or whether you want to start up a business based exclusively on Internet services.

You may have decided that Internet represents a cost-effective mechanism to market and sell your existing product or service to a new group of on-line consumers. The Internet represents the electronic equivalent of a global 1-800 telephone number which potential customers can use to browse Internet sites and purchase products and services. Or you may have chosen to be an active part of the Internet itself as an Internet growth business. As part of the Internet infrastructure, the entrepreneur is in a position to offer many new services and products to the large number of individuals who are joining, or who are already on, the Internet. The next two chapters present a wide array of possible business opportunities. Nontraditional businesses — businesses based on Internet services — are introduced and discussed in chapter 7.

For each business opportunity, Internet tools that can be used to support the opportunity are identified. When more than one Internet tool is applicable, the predominant services or mechanisms used are highlighted. See chapter 3 for a discussion of the Internet tools that form the basis on which a business can operate.

Internet can be a useful addition to many existing traditional businesses. However, it is unlikely to result in fantastic overnight changes to your business. The Internet primarily provides an additional vehicle with which to communicate with customers. The Internet can also be used to improve the competitiveness of an existing business by streamlining the flow of information within the business. Using the Internet as an adjunct to the traditional business enterprise should be viewed as an evolutionary, rather than revolutionary, step. In evaluating each of the business opportunities, you should keep in mind the complexity, cost, and available budget, as well as whether or not your business objectives would be met.

The entrepreneurial businessperson has the opportunity of using the Internet either actively or passively. For example, for a businessperson who favors a dynamic, leading-edge approach, the Internet can easily support a flashy multimedia catalogue, along with high-tech customer interaction and on-line ordering support mechanisms. For the more constrained businessperson, a less intensive approach limited to more static advertisements of existing product or service information, with no associated on-line ordering or feedback mechanisms, may be appropriate and more cost effective.

a. On-line electronic catalogues

A significant commercial use of the Internet has been catalogue-based selling. Catalogues range from simple text-based descriptions of items for sale to impressive on-line, interactive, multimedia presentations which may include color photos, animation, digital movies, and music, as well as built-in ordering capabilities. Sometimes a downloadable catalogue may be provided as an alternative or addition.

Electronic catalogues may be offered using almost any of the existing on-line Internet tools. There are numerous electronic catalogue approaches that exist, reflecting various budget, market, and technical choices. Some specific examples of how the electronic catalogues are currently being used on the Internet will be provided further on.

A key attraction of the electronic catalogue to customers is the convenience of being able to access it almost immediately,

How do on-line shopping patrons compare to home shopping patrons?
Home Shopping Network Interactive reports that 85% of purchases through Home Shopping Club TV are made by women, while 90% of on-line purchases are made by men. The average income of Home Shopping Network patrons is $45,000, while on-line shoppers' average income is $69,000.

and in some cases, the entertainment value that is provided as part of the presentation. An additional convenience that may appeal to environmentalists is the waste-free nature of the advertising medium. The key benefit to a business is that an electronic catalogue can reach a tremendous number of potential customers and is likely to cost significantly less than a printed catalogue to manufacture and distribute. Moreover, the content of electronic catalogues can easily be kept up to date.

The electronic catalogue format may be applied to virtually any type of merchandise. For example, the following types of merchandise are currently being sold on the Internet via electronic catalogue:

- Compact music discs
- Books and periodicals
- Personal items
- Entertainment event tickets
- Computer hardware and software
- Financial services
- Insurance
- Clothes
- Sporting goods
- Furniture
- Travel services
- Food
- Long distance telephone service
- Cars and automotive parts
- Airplanes and aircraft parts

Specialized merchandise-based business ventures, which lend themselves to mail-order delivery, may have the most to gain from the Internet. But no matter how eclectic or specialized the service or product a business markets, there will be users on the Internet who will find the business offering of interest.

Overview of on-line purchases*

- Software, hardware, books, music, and vacation/travel are the most popular on-line purchases.
- Apparel is the least purchased item.
- On-line buying is more common for less expensive products than for more expensive products.
- Web spending increased 35% from 1994 to 1995.
- Growth of on-line shopping depends on vendor reliability and security.
- Legal services are of little interest.

*GTRC 1995 survey

Electronic catalogues can vary dramatically in terms of style, content, and image. In terms of basic capabilities, electronic catalogues commonly allow the user to select various products displayed and then automatically print out a completed order form which may then be mailed or faxed to the business. Some companies have included animation, digital video, music, and, in some cases, have actually integrated the catalogue into entertainment software in an attempt to draw attention. Making catalogue use an enjoyable experience will increase the catalogue's popularity among potential customers.

A key element to consider when developing your electronic catalogue is that not every user will have access to multimedia capabilities on their computer (e.g., sound cards and graphics display monitors). Consequently, your business will need to make a difficult choice: appeal to everyone or appeal to a subset of users.

There are several options of Internet services that support an electronic catalogue. The simplest approach — the method which requires minimal support on the part of the business in terms of technical skill or Internet resources — is to provide an e-mail info-server. As described in chapter 3, an e-mail info-server supports automatic responses to any e-mail messages it receives. In this particular application, the autoresponder provides the user with the business's electronic catalogue: a text-only letter providing a listing of product or service descriptions, prices, and ordering information. The benefit of this approach to the businessperson is the simplicity and low cost. The benefit to the customer is that all he or she needs to receive this information is a computer and e-mail access. No special graphics displays or high-end computer are required, unlike other Internet services such as the Web.

The businessperson offering an e-mail based catalogue should be aware of certain Internet customer sensitivities. Some Internet users are sensitive to the size of files that are sent by e-mail because of limitations in various software packages. Other Internet customers may be concerned about charges they accrue that are based on the size and number of e-mail messages they receive and store on-line with their ISP, BBS, or OSP. If your catalogue is likely to exceed more than a couple of typed pages, you should consider the alternative approaches that are described below.

> **Quality of information***
> - 89% of users feel quality of information is a major issue on the Internet.
> - Users seek more detailed information about more expensive products than less expensive products.
>
> **GTRC 1995 survey*

With a large volume of information, you should provide an easy method for your customer to access and search an on-line electronic catalogue. The easiest way to do this is to offer a method such as FTP, Gopher, WAIS, or the Web for the customer to connect to a designated Internet address and browse a catalogue containing brief descriptions, prices, and ordering information. You might also allow users to select items and place an order on-line.

Another approach is to use Telnet, which has the benefit of ensuring that the catalogue is available to most Internet users. This is achieved through the limitation of the Telnet tool, which restricts the catalogue presentation to a text-only format (e.g., no special graphics or photos). To access the electronic catalogue, the customers use Telnet to access the designated Internet address. The Internet address connects customers to your business site where they can interact dynamically with your electronic catalogue.

You also have various options for presenting the information in your catalogue to the customer. A simple browsing tool may be provided that allows the customer to move around by making menu choices. Alternatively, you might allow the customer to perform searches of the electronic catalogue for specific phrases or keywords.

Another popular method for reaching a wide range of Internet users takes advantage of FTP. FTP is used to disseminate catalogues that Internet users download and use on their computers. For multimedia-type catalogues, using FTP may involve working with a software consultant who will prepare the content and features you desire, or using a commercially available catalogue preparation program (such as Prostar's Minicat) to create the catalogue yourself. Once it is complete, you will have a computer file that contains your catalogue. In order to make it available to Internet users, you must put the catalogue file on one or more anonymous FTP sites.

Gopher can also be used to provide on-line browsable, electronic catalogues. However, the use of the Gopher tool is being quickly superseded by text-based and graphic-based Web browsers. Because of this, we don't recommend using Gopher as a basis for anything other than distributing a downloadable electronic catalogue.

Internet presences using Telnet

Book Stacks Unlimited
telnet://books.com

CD Now!
telnet://cdnow.com

Compact Disc Connection
telnet://cdconnection.com/

Flower Link
telnet://flowerlink.com

Traders' Connection
telnet://trader.com

Video Express
telnet://videoexpress.com

Internet presences using FTP

Compact Disc Connection
ftp://ftp.cdconnection.com/

Internet presences using Gopher

Addison-Wesley
gopher://aw.com/

WAIS is also a good tool for large catalogues where a good searching capability would be attractive to customers and where graphical content is not a major selling factor of the product or service. One of the benefits of WAIS is that it can be readily integrated into Web-based or Telnet catalogues.

If your product or service relies on customers viewing it, or if your product or service may be purchased by customers with limited technical knowledge or interest, the most promising method for electronic catalogue merchandising is a Web page. As discussed in chapter 3, the Web provides a great deal of flexibility when it comes to formatting and presenting graphical and text information to on-line customers. Further, the Web can be used to present customers with on-line order forms. Generally, using the Web is a much simpler activity than using any of the other Internet services, and may appeal to a wider range of casual Internet users.

Internet presences using the Web

Book Stacks Unlimited
http://www.books.com

Bookport
http://www.bookport.com

b. *One-on-one customer communications*

The Internet provides a unique opportunity for a business to interact one on one with its existing customer base if the customer already has access to the Internet via e-mail. Internet e-mail allows customers to interact with the business over distance and outside normal office hours. Neither the business nor customer is necessarily bound by the physical location of the other when it comes to transacting business, and e-mail also allows both the customer and the business person to circumvent "telephone tag."

Using e-mail for customer correspondence can also lead to savings for the business in terms of clerical support and mailing costs. For some businesses and clients, savings may also be realized if the information exchanged does not need to be re-entered into a spreadsheet or word processor program.

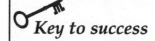

Key to success

Home-based business +
Internet = Good idea
Internet-based selling can reduce or eliminate the need to maintain office space and is well suited to home-based businesses.

c. *Sales support*

Sales support can be implemented using varying degrees of automation or personnel-based approaches. One option would be to allow individuals to send a request to an e-mail info-server which would send back a pre-prepared information. The type of information that may be included in such a message is not constrained and might include a product or service list, price list, business location and directions, current sale information, business background, specific product descriptions, ordering

*Prepacked information
on the Internet*

Joe Boxer
mailto:joeboxer@joeboxer.com
http://www.joeboxer.com

information, and product reviews or testimonials. This approach can be further enhanced by including a note with an e-mail address to which the customer can send queries not addressed by the pre-prepared information.

The other extreme would be to provide an automated quote system, based on the Gopher, Web, or Telnet tools, that would allow a customer to type in specific details and receive an on-line customized quote.

d. After-sales product or service support

Businesses that provide after-sales support to their customers, either by toll-free or local telephone service or via traditional mail, may find that the Internet provides them with a low-cost method to work with customers. This service can take many different forms ranging from the very simple to the very sophisticated. The key benefit that the Internet offers is the ability to provide customer support 24 hours of the day, 365 days of the year. The Internet may also, depending on how it is used, significantly reduce the support effort required.

The simplest after-sales support service using the Internet is an e-mail address to which customers can direct information requests and issues. If your business requires product registration for warranty purposes, you can design the service to allow the customer to send an e-mail registration. Alternatively, an e-mail info-server service could be offered which provides troubleshooting tips or information on local customer service centers.

A potential side benefit of the customer support line is that it may be used for customers to sign up for an e-mail mailing list for registered products and follow-up surveys on customer satisfaction. It is important to note that customers should be the ones who determine if they will receive e-mailings from your business (see chapter 3). To a limited degree, you can also use e-mail addresses to provide demographic information for your business.

Customer support may be tailored to suit the needs of your business's on-line customers and products or services. The Telnet tool can be used to enable customers to connect to a text-based computer program that provides them with access to information including commonly asked questions, troubleshooting tips, product specifications, authorized service center locations, business hours, and customer feedback facilities. Many businesses currently run dial-up BBSs that provide this type of electronic customer support. Some large companies provide a toll-free dial-up access, while others leave the customer to pay for any related toll-access fees.

The Web can also function in the same way as Telnet. The Web approach offers significantly more flexibility in terms of being able to present interactive diagrams which can assist with parts ordering and troubleshooting.

Depending on the nature of the product or service your business offers, there may be a benefit in providing a Usenet newsgroup or e-mail discussion group that would allow customers to interact among themselves to discuss topics of common interest. This approach would be particularly applicable for businesses that have a large base of customers with Internet access. It is interesting to note that for some products, the users themselves will start up a Usenet newsgroup. If a newsgroup related to your company already exists, after-sales support can be improved by monitoring customer discussions on new ideas for improvements. Issues affecting customer satisfaction may also be anticipated and addressed.

e. Corporate presence

All companies strive to put information that meets the company's need to define itself, attract customers or investors, and satisfy the needs of shareholders into the hands of potential customers and shareholders. With the Internet, there is now also an underlying desire by some companies to be associated with new areas of technology and to be considered as leading edge in the industry.

An increasing number of corporations have been using the Internet as a means to gain market presence or to increase consumer awareness of their products or services, market performance, or corporate goals. Some companies also use the Internet to highlight their attractiveness as a workplace for prospective employees.

To date, the Web has been the principal vehicle used to perform corporate marketing, primarily providing multimedia information sources for browsing by Internet users. For example, Nortel, a large telecommunications manufacturer, has taken a proactive approach to the Internet. Nortel provides a typical Internet

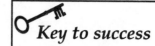

Key to success

Eliminate toll charge barriers for your customers

If your business already has a BBS for sales support or customer service, you should consider connecting it to the Internet. By using the Internet as an access medium rather than dial-up access, you can reduce the costs associated with 1-800 fees while simultaneously making your business's on-line sales support or customer service globally accessible.

Companies providing customer support on the Internet

Dell Computers
http://www.dell.com/techinfo

Hewlett Packard
http://support.mayfield.hp.com/

Corporate presences on the Internet

Citibank
http://www.citibank.com

MCI
http://www.mci.com

Microsoft
http://www.microsoft.com

Northern Telecom (Nortel)
http://www.nt.com

Silicon Graphics
http://www.sgi.com

Time Warner
http://www.timeinc.com

presence for a large corporation in that it provides information on corporate objectives, performance, and news releases. However, Nortel also provides details on environmental issues and initiatives in which it is involved, with the intention of presenting its objectives to similarly interested individuals. The Nortel site is also bilingual.

Nonprofit organizations have taken advantage of the Internet's reach as well: an on-line presence lets them do so. The Internet is an inexpensive way to provide information on an organization's goals, initiatives, and accomplishments to a wide audience and may secure support both in principle and financially. An on-line site helps keep organization members and supporters in closer touch, with less expense than periodic post mailings ever could.

Cities and tourist boards have also been quick to realize the global nature of the Internet, and many have set up information sites using Internet facilities. Information sites have been established to promote business opportunities and tourism. Some sites go beyond static information by including regularly updated video clips or photos that can be downloaded and viewed by potential visitors.

f. Product or service advertising

If the demographics of the Internet-user community match the target market of your product or service, you may want to consider advertising on the Internet. The Internet can be used for advertising in a manner similar to print advertisement. Internet advertising provides the same potential benefits to the business and consumer that nonInternet advertising does, but also offers some additional benefits since it can be customized to the customer and updated as required.

Internet advertising can also be used as an enhancement to print advertisements, business cards, letterhead, and product packaging. An Internet address included as part of a print advertisement provides potential customers with an avenue to obtain additional information which is more detailed and perhaps more current than that of the original print ad.

Where and how do you advertise on the Internet? Just as with any form of advertising, it is important that both the audience and the incentive, or "draw," to view the advertising are there. It is also important to note that, as with radio and television,

Nonprofit organizations on the Internet

Amnesty International
http://www.io.org/amnesty/ overview.html

National Rifle Association
http://www.nra.org

Cities and tourist boards on the Internet

British Columbia, Canada
http://www.tbc.gov.bc.ca/tourism/ tourismhome.html

Charlotte, North Carolina
http://www.hickory.nc.us/ncnetworks/ clt-intrl.html

Los Angeles, California
http://www.ci.la.ca.us

City Net
http://www.city.net/

potential customers can turn off the advertising and go elsewhere with the click of a button. This means that the user is not forced to view any unwanted advertising.

Simply setting up a Web site for your business that includes straight advertising copy is unlikely to attract many potential customers by itself. Advertising is often associated with places where people are likely to gather, such as sporting events and bus-stop shelters. On the Internet, one way to gather potential customers is by providing useful information or entertainment. To keep a steady flow of potential customers, it is important to keep the information content fresh and to ensure that your site continues to stand out from similar sites.

There are three main Internet tools that may be used for advertising, the most predominate being the Web. The ease of use for potential customers and the publication facilities of the Web are the key reasons for its popularity. However, popular Web sites can charge more than $10,000 a month for advertising space, placing them out of reach of many small businesses.

The other tools that are used to lesser degrees are e-mail and Usenet newsgroups. It is a common misconception that Usenet is off limits for business. However, both e-mail and Usenet newsgroups are potentially counterproductive when used for advertising and must be used with care. Chapter 8 discusses how these tools can be used for general advertising purposes and identifies the pitfalls.

For software products, Internet advertising can be used in conjunction with Internet distribution of demonstration versions of the software. Two such examples are the very popular Netscape Navigator (a Web browser), and Gazzillionaire (a computer game).

The Internet can also be used to distribute electronic knick-knacks. Just as businesses distribute small gifts with their logo and other business information on them, the Internet provides you with the potential to distribute special software programs that have entertainment and advertising value combined. Such programs can be based on short games, screen savers, and animation. Ford Motor Company has used this approach. Ford distributes a program that allows the user to test drive a new car in a video game format, and then gives the customer the option to fill out an order sheet and determine expected retail cost of the car.

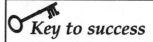

Key to success

Big bang for the buck

You can use the Internet to reach a much more global audience than you could with any paper publication, and at a significantly reduced cost. For example, a typical direct mailing of 10,000 advertisements in the United States or Canada may cost upward of a few thousand dollars. The same coverage on the Internet, using the Web, costs only about $20 a month and a few hundred dollars in initial authoring fees. Your business doesn't need to have any direct contact with the Internet, as everything may be set up through a consultant. You can purchase Internet advertising as you would an ad in the local newspaper, without needing to know how to use the Internet.

Companies advertising on the Internet

Coca-Cola
http://www.cocacola.com/

Digital Computer Corporation
http://www.digital.com/

Levi Strauss & Co.
http://www.levi.com/

MasterCard International, Inc
http://www.mastercard.com/

Volvo
http://www.volvocars.com/

g. Customer order tracking

Customers like to be kept informed and often want to know the status of their accounts or outstanding orders. The ability to instantly satisfy this need can be readily supported over the Internet using any of the Internet tools. However, the Web, with its support for forms, form submission, and security transaction options seems to be the best tool.

If status information is readily available on an existing computer system, implementing an Internet-based customer order tracking system can help reduce business overhead by reducing the number of personnel required to staff customer service telephones. A good example of such an application on the Internet is Federal Express, which maintains a Web site that allows customers to track the progress of their packages by entering their waybill number.

h. Custom research support

The Internet provides access to numerous information sources. For example, the Internet enables you to monitor industry trends, assess competitors, obtain background information on potential customers, obtain government and supplier information, solicit customer feedback, and even obtain financial or investment information. Research on the Internet is primarily supported by WAIS, Gopher, Web, and Telnet tools.

Pay-per-use Internet information resources are also emerging. These services differentiate themselves from the free services by their comprehensive and organized nature. The services range from customized news clipping to specialized databases on taxation, banking, and international laws, all of which may prove useful to your business operation and marketing strategy. Fee structures vary widely.

Business tip:
Subscribe to a news clipping service!

News clipping services are offered by several on-line companies and can be a very powerful business tool. A news clipping service will regularly scan news wires and various on-line databases for keywords specified by the subscriber. The subscriber is often given the option of specifying several "profiles" against which to perform regular searches. All articles that are found matching the keywords are e-mailed to the subscriber.

We took advantage of one of the pay-per-use on-line services called San Jose Mercury News Newshound in order to keep current on what was being said about the Internet in the media. We found the Newshound service was a very cost-effective method of keeping informed of what was being written in the newspapers across the United States. The service costs $4.95 a month and allows you to specify up to five profiles.

To help us track on-line activities, we set up one profile which had Newshound look for all articles that had any of the following terms present: Online, on-line, Prodigy, Compuserve, e-World, America Online, AOL, Internet, Information Superhighway, and Cyberspace. Every hour, the Newshound software checked articles available on several newswire services such as Associated Press, as well as those of large urban newspapers, including the *Chicago Tribune*. Newshound then sent by e-mail the full text of any article matching our news clipping profile.

We highly recommend this type of service to any business that uses information found in the newspapers as input into its decision-making processes!

Pay-per-use Internet information resources

Dialog
http://www.dialog.com

Dow Jones Business Information Services
http://dowvision.wais.net

Encyclopedia Britannica
http://www.eb.com

LEXIS-NEXIS
http://www.lexis-nexis.com

Newshound
http://www.sjmercury.com/
mailto:newshound@sjmercury.com

i. Employee recruitment

Employee recruitment is definitely one area where the Internet provides an advantage to anyone who wants to hire professionally skilled employees or for professionals looking for work. Human resource companies, primarily those specializing in matching skilled jobs with candidates, have set up shop on the Internet, using Web and Gopher tools. These services typically

Employee recruitment services on the Internet

Monster Board
http://www.monster.com

Online Career Center
http://www.occ.com/occ

E-SPAN's Interactive Employment Network
http://www.espan.com/

*Usenet newsgroups providing
employee recruitment*

news:misc.jobs.offered
(position announcements)

news:biz.jobs.offered
(position announcements)

news:misc.jobs.resumes
(for posting resumes)

news:misc.jobs.contract
(contract position announcements)

provide a database of available positions in an attempt to entice potential candidates. Specialized BBSs and large OSPs provide various types of job and employee search functions. One of the issues surrounding these services is that their viewing is limited to customers of the specific systems. The Internet's global reach can't be matched and is ideal for a business looking to staff open positions, particularly positions requiring hard-to-match or in-demand skills.

The Usenet is another good tool for recruitment. Posting job announcements in appropriate Usenet newsgroups is very easy and is regularly done by many companies.

When looking for newsgroups in which to post job announcements or find a position, you should also look for appropriate regional newsgroups. A regional newsgroup is one that is distributed only, and usually accessible only, within a city, state, province, or country. Your ISP can help you identify regional newsgroups appropriate to your needs.

j. *Electronic tender and bidding*

Electronic tender and bidding

Open bidding service
(Information Systems
Management Corporation)
http://www.obs.ism.ca/
mailto:information@obs.obs.ism.ca

Heavy construction tenders
(Explorer Software)
http://www.explorer-software.com/

Global Business
Opportunities Services
(U.S. Department of Commerce,
Economics and Statistics)
http://www.stat-usa.gov/BEN/
Services/globus.html

Trade Opportunity Program
(University of Michigan)
gopher://una.hh.lib.umich.edu:
70/11/ebb/top

University of New Brunswick
http://degaulle.hil.unb.ca/
UNB_G_Services/tenders.html

If you regularly post tenders or receive business through tenders, the use of the Internet can be a very effective adjunct to your business. Government agencies are currently publicizing tenders and trade leads on the Internet. The Internet can be used to distribute tenders to interested vendors or to increase your awareness of available tenders.

The Web, e-mail, and Gopher are currently the most popular tools being used for this purpose. There are various electronic bidding and tender systems currently on the Internet. Information Systems Management Corporation offers an open bidding service on the Web that lists business opportunities in various Canadian governmental agencies and public sector organizations. Explorer Software offers a directory to on-line tenders related to the construction industry, and the Global Business Opportunities Services provides a listing of government-issued procurement opportunities for U.S. businesses from the U.S. Department of Commerce, Economics and Statistics. The Trade Opportunity Program from the University of Michigan provides daily information on government and international agency tenders, while the University of New Brunswick offers on-line printing and desktop publishing related tenders.

k. Electronic publishing

The Internet is the basis for a coming revolution in publishing. It provides the means to simplify the electronic production and distribution of news, advertising fliers, newsletters, journals, and even books. The Internet opens the door for you to enter the publishing business with minimal overhead for manufacturing, marketing, distribution, or sales. Standard document distribution formats such as Portable Document Format (PDF), coupled with applications such as Adobe Acrobat that allow viewing and printing of these documents on any type of computer, enable you to make relatively complex presentations. Any of the Internet tools can provide the mechanism for marketing, distribution, and sales.

Electronic news services are very powerful because of their immediacy and potential for customization. Several companies on the Internet are currently offering such services. One company, ClariNet, offers an electronic newswire. ClariNet takes a vast number of news articles from newspapers and other sources, and makes them available in private Usenet newsgroups. These newsgroups may be viewed only, and don't support any general article postings from users. The newsgroups' topics range from weather to regional information. ClariNet charges BBSs and ISPs a fee to receive these newsgroups. The BBSs and ISPs then make these newsgroups available to their subscribers, usually for a fee.

Some companies offer the subscribers the option of either electronic or paper subscriptions. For instance, *Internet Week*, published by Phillips Business Information, is offered electronically to subscribers using the Web tool — for $99 less than the paper version.

For journals or periodicals, particularly those targeted at telecommunications or computer professionals, the Internet is a particularly viable medium and its use is expected to increase. However, while it is unlikely that the Internet will ever replace print media, it is very synergistic. For example, CMP Publications and Time Warner both use the Web tool to provide tables of contents and selected articles from popular magazines that are available for general browsing by the Internet community. The purpose of this sort of site is to entice new customers to purchase the magazine on the newsstand or by subscription. The information sites provide details on how to subscribe to the magazines, either electronically or by mail, telephone, or fax.

Electronic distribution of books

Dial-A-Book, Inc.
http://dab.psi.net/DialABook/

Electronic current news publications

ClariNet
http://www.clarinet.com/

Newspage
http://www.newspage.com/

San Jose Mercury News
http://www.sjmercury.com/

USA Today
http://www.usatoday.com/

Phillips Business Information
http://www.phillips.com/iw

CMP Publications
http://techweb.cmp.com

Time Warner
http://www.pathfinder.com/

Business tip:
Portable document format

There is a multitude of word processing applications existing today, each with its own file formats. Each type of computer system (e.g., PC, Macintosh, Unix) tends to have its own special word processing applications and file formats. This diversity of file formats used to store documents presents a significant barrier to general electronic distribution of documents that include anything but the most basic text formatting.

Recently, a standard document file format known as portable document format (PDF) has emerged. PDF is particularly noteworthy because it allows a document to preserve its embedded graphics, fonts, and special formatting, regardless of which computer system the document is viewed or printed from.

Adobe is the industry leader in PDF technology, and sells programs that allow you to generate and edit documents stored in this format. Adobe provides a freeware program for most computer systems that allows you to view and print out such documents, making PDF a very attractive method of distributing documents to the Internet community.

Adobe Systems Incorporated
1585 Charleston Road
P.O. Box 7900
Mountain View, CA 94039-7900
1-800-862-3623, 1-800-833-6687
http://www.adobe.com/

E-zines

Good Medicine Magazine
http://none.coolware.com/health/ good_med/ThisIssue.html

HotWired
http://www.hotwired.com

International Teletimes
http://www.teletimes.com

John Labovitz's E-ZINE LIST
http://www.meer.net/~johnl/ e-zine-list/index.html

A phenomenon on the Internet is the growth of on-line electronic magazines, or *e-zines* as they are generally referred to. Today, there are over 400 e-zines published on the Internet, some for profit, others for personal pleasure. Some e-zines, such as *HotWired*, are published by businesses; others are published by individuals, such as *International Teletimes*, published exclusively on the Web by a university student in Vancouver.

E-zines may be presented and distributed in several forms to Internet users, from a simple text file that is transferred using e-mail or FTP to multimedia entertainment using the Web.

For publishers, the Internet provides a unique opportunity to collect leads and obtain source information from individuals "on the scene" in remote countries, using e-mail. E-mail can be considered the equivalent of a global toll-free telephone number. *International Teletimes*, for example, is produced almost entirely through e-mail.

The Internet can also be used to stimulate customer interest in new books and to make potential customers aware of the publisher's product line. Companies such as McGraw-Hill and Prentice Hall make sample chapters of new books available on the Internet. Some publishers also offer direct sales to the customer through the Internet.

Another method to stimulate customer interest in new books is to use existing Usenet newsgroups to present reviews and announcements of new books. Based on general Usenet advertising guidelines, it may be appropriate for a publisher or author to post a brief notice; check the newsgroup's FAQ and act accordingly. Some of the Usenet newsgroups welcome advertising from publishers while some do not, although third-party book reviews may usually be posted with permission. Authors and publishers also usually have the option of responding to posted reviews about their work. As well, some Usenet newsgroups have FAQs listing publisher-related information to which publishers may add by contacting the FAQ authors.

l. Distributorships

For a business that wishes to grow, the Internet enables you to easily solicit distributors or resellers in other cities or countries. Traditional methods might involve buying advertising in newspapers or trade magazines of the appropriate city or country. With the Internet, you can simply post a query on an appropriate Usenet newsgroup, stating your business name, type of product or service, and area in which a distributor is needed. Another method is to post to a relevant e-mail discussion list.

Likewise, if you are actively looking for additional products which you can distribute, finding and monitoring the appropriate newsgroup or mailing list can be to your advantage. The global reach of the Internet is a real advantage to this type of

Book publishers on the Internet

Addison-Wesley
gopher://aw.com/
http://www.aw.com/

Macmillan Computer Publishing
http://www.mcp.com

McGraw-Hill
gopher://mcgraw.infor.com:5000/

Penguin Books USA, Inc.
http://www.penguin.com/usa/

Prentice Hall
http://www.prenhall.com

Self-Counsel Press
http://www.swifty.com/scp/

Publisher directories

Title Net
http//www.infor.com

Oxford University
*http://www.comlab.ox.ac.uk/
archive/publishers.html*

Usenet newsgroups of reviews and book announcements

news:alt.books.reviews

news:biz.books.technical

news:alt.books.technical

news:rec.arts.books

news:misc.books.technical

business activity. Follow-up discussions can also be economically held using e-mail.

m. Raising investment funds

The Internet should be considered as a conduit through which potential investors can be reached and enticed. Information on public offerings or corporate performance may be made available on the Internet using the Web, Gopher, and e-mail. Using any of the techniques discussed in chapter 8, the site can be made visible to the Internet community; interested users will visit your Internet resource to review the information you present.

In the July/August 1995 issue of *Success* magazine, an article by Jenny McCune presented an example of the Internet being used in such a way. The Spring Street Brewing Company had posted information on its upcoming public offering on a Web site. The Web site attracted tens of thousands of potential investors. Spring Street Brewing considered the Web site a very cost-effective advertising method, having invested $200 for the Web site setup and $150 per month to keep it going.

Spring Street Brewing Company
http://plaza.interport.net/witbeer/

n. Personal networking and business resource

As a personal business resource, the Internet is unparalleled. The Internet provides government information, contacts and e-mail addresses, discussion groups for self-help, practical and theoretical discussions of business, information on professional societies, financial information, and personal networking. It might be difficult to discuss business problems with local competitors, but having access to other business professionals who don't represent a competitive threat can be of benefit to you.

The Internet community revels in the free exchange of information and ideas. The two primary tools used for this are e-mail discussion groups and Usenet newsgroups. You are sure to find a topical discussion relevant to your interests and needs. Some people who participate on mailing lists take advantage of industry conferences to set up face-to-face, or "birds of a feather" meetings to discuss topics of common interest. It is not necessary to know the discussion group's members and no invitation is required — everyone is welcome to participate. All that is asked is that your participation be consistent with the rules laid out by the FAQ for a Usenet newsgroup and by the mailing list owner or moderator for e-mail discussion groups. To find out what mailing lists and newsgroups are available, see the Internet resources discussed in chapter 4 and listed in the appendix.

o. Business communication

1. Providing support to salesreps

Through e-mail, salesreps on the road can be kept informed of price changes and sales status. They can draw on the resources of their company computers by using Telnet to gain access to customer data and sales support programs (e.g., automated quote and inventory applications). Salesreps may also use e-mail to avoid telephone tag, coordinate with home-office personnel, and generally take care of paperwork. Since e-mail never sleeps, messages can be composed and sent outside of the company's normal working hours — forwarded to the recipients before they arrive at work the next morning. The benefit of e-mail to the home office is that a single message can be sent simultaneously to all salespersons with the push of a button. Through the use of third-party e-mail services, urgent e-mail messages can automatically generate a page to the e-mail recipient.

2. Interoffice communication

Every business that has more than one location inevitably has a need for interoffice communication to coordinate day-to-day business activities. For a business with locations in different cities or countries, coordination by telephone can be a hit-and-miss proposition. For a business that is already computerized, integration of the Internet e-mail into the general fabric of the business's operation is a simple initiative that may have good payback.

3. Long distance voice communication

In 1994, a small company called VocalTec developed a shareware software application that allows two people connected to the Internet to have voice communication in a manner similar to using a telephone. The software operates on 486 IBM PC compatibles running Windows 3.1 with an inexpensive sound card, microphone, and minimum 14.4Kbps modem SLIP/PPP connection to the Internet. The program uses voice compression technology and the Internet to allow computer users to talk

Long distance voice communication

Electric Magic Company
http://www.emagic.com

Third Planet Publishing
http://www.ikon.com/digiphone/

VocalTec
http://www.vocaltec.com

between cities at the cost of only a local telephone call to their ISPs.

The Electric Magic Company has recently come out with a similar application for Macintosh computers. Other companies can be expected to offer similar and enhanced software programs in the near future.

4. Desktop video conferencing

Have you ever been on the telephone with one of your peers or staff at a remote location and wondered what his or her exact facial expression was? Have you ever wondered if everyone on a conference call was really paying attention to the discussion, or if they were actually doing something other than participating in the call? The solution to this is desktop video conferencing, which allows you to see videos of the person you are talking with, in small windows on your computer screen.

Professional video conferencing can cost thousands of dollars just for the equipment. If you are willing to live with lower detail resolution and slower update rates, you may want to consider trying desktop video conferencing using the Internet. If you already have a 386 PC with 28.8 Kbps SLIP/PPP connection to the Internet, you have the ability to have desktop video conferencing with your remote business sites. Using a PC, you will need to spend only about $100 for a small camera from Connectix, called Quickcam. Then, with the installation of freeware software from Cornell University called CU-SeeMe, you will be ready to go!

Desktop video conferencing

CU-SeeMe
ftp://gated.cornell.edu/pub/CU-SeeMe/

Connectix
http://www.connectix.com/

With the CU-SeeMe software, you will be able to set up a one-on-one video conference or a multiperson video conference. The quality of the images you receive will vary, depending on the power of the computer, video equipment of the conference participants, speed of the Internet connection, and network congestion on the "information superhighway" between the conference sites.

A video conferencing setup can also be used to monitor if anyone is present at a particular remote location. The relatively low resolution that the equipment provides does not allow for more detailed surveillance however.

5. Electronic data interchange

Electronic data interchange, or EDI, means doing business without exchanging paper documents between companies. EDI is accomplished by exchanging electronic documents between company computer systems. Electronic documents can include, but are not limited to, things such as purchase orders, invoices, and inventory reports. The electronic documents are very formalized and usually conform to a particular national or international standard.

EDI is slowly moving from large businesses to small businesses. EDI techniques have been credited with reducing the business cycle by removing paper and associated manual processing from transactions between companies, and EDI interest has been steadily increasing. The U.S. government has been a major force behind federal agencies making more extensive use of EDI to streamline government processes and reduce costs. EDI between companies has typically required proprietary software and subscription fees to large EDI clearing-house services that manage the exchange of data between associated businesses.

While the Internet provides a cost-effective medium for remote business sites to exchange electronic data, Internet applications are not quite ready to support standard EDI applications. However, for enterprising businesses, a simplistic approach to EDI can be readily accomplished within the business and with trusted or key business partners. Purchase orders, shipping notification, and invoices can be transmitted using Internet tools such as e-mail and FTP. Where security is required, existing encryption tools (such as Pretty Good Privacy, described in chapter 5) can be used.

Internet EDI resources

Directory of EDI providers, services, organizations, and other EDI resources provided by Unidex (Unidex, Inc)
http://www.wwa.com/unidex/edi/

Electronic commerce resource guide (Premenos)
http://www.premenos.com/

7.

Nontraditional business opportunities

The large number of value-added and service-oriented businesses that have developed for the telecommunications industry will blossom to sustain Internet as well. A completely new set of businesses have emerged over the years, whose primary purpose is to help other companies make the best use of the telephone for their business. Fax-on-demand service bureaus are just one example.

The Internet presents numerous opportunities for infrastructure, consumer, and value-added type businesses. Some opportunities are speculative, others already have a demonstrated market demand. While a step-by-step analysis of what is required to set up business in each of these areas is beyond the scope of this book, this chapter will give you an idea of what opportunities you may wish to pursue further. Some opportunities require a modest investment in computer equipment, and most require a moderate to high degree of technical knowledge.

Each opportunity is rated on a scale of one to five one representing the least amount of knowledge and skills needed. The ratings given are the lowest we feel is necessary. The technical requirements of each level, or what may be involved in the opportunities rated at this level, are explained in Table #7. (Ratings of one to five are represented by computer icons: ⌨)

TABLE #7
RATING SYSTEM FOR BUSINESS OPPORTUNITIES
IN CHAPTER 7

🖥️	• Knowledge of connecting to the Internet and using associated tools • May involve preparing HTML Web pages (see chapter 8)
🖥️🖥️	🖥️ **+ programming skills** • Ability to program using high-level programming language such as Visual BASIC or C/C++ • May require understanding of Internet protocols • May involve programming CGI scripts for Web pages
🖥️🖥️🖥️	🖥️🖥️ **+ computer system administration skills** (e.g., Unix system administrator) • Ability to set up and administer out-of-box computer system and data communications equipment • Ability to set up and manage out-of-box software applications
🖥️🖥️🖥️🖥️	🖥️🖥️🖥️ **+ system integration skills** • Ability to take existing software and/or hardware and "glue" them together to provide a specific capability (e.g., writing software programs or preparing special cables to connect equipment)
🖥️🖥️🖥️🖥️🖥️	🖥️🖥️🖥️🖥️ **+ specialized skills** • Ability to set up and administer equipment more complex than a single computer and software (e.g., routers, local area networks) • May require extensive knowledge of computer networks other than the Internet • May require specialized troubleshooting skills • May require programming of specialized computer applications

a. Information services

Information services represent a potentially explosive growth area for Internet entrepreneurs. Internet users thrive on information of any sort, and the Internet provides an inexpensive method to deliver information to these users anywhere. You only have to look at the large OSPs and the success of France's Minitel service to realize that there is a demand and that information services can be profitable enterprises. Information services can be, and are being, offered using Web, WAIS, and Telnet applications.

Willingness to pay fees for information services *
- 67.3% Yes
- 22.6% No

*GTRC 1995 Survey

Business tip:
Minitel success

France has a well-established on-line service that has been in operation for over 15 years. The service is run by France Telecom and has many private companies offering services. Minitel has over 6.5 million access terminals in active use and offers over 25,000 services catering to a diverse set of business and personal needs.

Minitel services are tariffed by the minute. Minitel is profitable for both France Telecom and service providers alike. In 1994, Minitel brought in 6.6 billion francs, of which 3.1 billion was paid out to Minitel service providers. If you are interested in more information on Minitel, send e-mail to *info@minitel.fr* .

---

1. Consumer-oriented information services

Examples of information services that could be provided include:

- Airline schedule and routing information
- Alumni directories for colleges and universities
- Astrological information
- Collectibles price lists (e.g., coins, stamps, books, comics)
- College and university information
- Community services
- Consumer product reports
- Event calendars, community bulletins

- Family law, small business law
- Farmers' almanac
- Financial information (e.g., stocks, mutual funds, mortgage rates, GIC and RRSP daily rate information, tax tips)
- Gardening
- Genealogical information
- General education-oriented databases geared toward high school students
- Government information (e.g., local, regional, federal)
- Hobby information
- Horse racing statistics
- How-to information for homeowners
- Insurance policies, rates, brokers
- Internet resources indexes
- Local classified ads
- Lottery information
- Movie/video reviews
- Music charts
- News, current events
- Non-traditional medical remedies
- Yellow Pages database
- Pharmaceutical database for prescription drugs
- Police/crime information
- Postal code database
- Price comparison database for local stores
- Product safety and recalls
- Public transit routes and schedules
- Recipes, menu planning
- Rental/realty property
- Road conditions
- Soap opera news and gossip

Information services

Muse (stock digital photos)
http://www.weststock.com

Cognito (family and consumer information resources)
http://www.cognito.com

Health Gate (medical and health information)
http://www.healthgate.com

- Sporting event calendars
- Sports scores and historical statistics
- Travel and tourist information
- Weather

It is difficult to say which, if any, of these services will be the "killer information service," but it is a good bet that personal finance information will be among the top runners. Personal finance services lend themselves well to computer user needs, as financial management is often done by computer owners.

2. Business-oriented information services

Business needs for information encompass information topics such as:

- Business law
- Business regulations, bylaws
- Company profiles
- Competitive data
- Current news
- Demographic information
- Foreign culture and business etiquette
- Franchise directory and profiles
- Job tenders database
- Mailing lists
- Office equipment troubleshooting
- Professional conference calendar
- Professional services directory
- Standards (e.g., telecommunication, consumer, government, local, international)
- Stock media for publishing (e.g., graphics, photos, video)
- Stock and financial information
- Tax information
- Tenders and business opportunities
- Trade show and conference calendars

- Travel schedules

- Yellow Pages listings for suppliers, distributors, and consultants

Business-information services can range from databases that can be searched using ad hoc English-like search requests to automated information "culling" services that are always searching though new information and generating customized reports to subscribers based on pre-defined interest profiles.

b. Entertainment

On-line entertainment is a feature of OSPs and BBSs and has a strong following in the Internet community. Multiplayer games are particularly popular.

OSPs tend to offer very polished multiplayer games with high-quality graphics and entertainment value. BBSs tend toward mundane text-based or low-resolution graphics-type games. Popular user-created games on the Internet are text-based, multiplayer adventure games. Internet games have names such as MUDs and MOOS, and immerse the player in a virtual reality of fantasy that is populated by both computer-controlled and human-controlled players. The games can provide a very intense, addictive playing experience.

The Internet provides a mechanism to both deliver software games to the customer and provide the method to support multiplayer gaming. Vendors such as Microprose have been quick to recognize the great potential of the Internet to support multiplayer gaming. Microprose recently released an Internet version of its popular game "Sid Meier's Civilization," called "Sid Meier's CIVNet." Other multiplayer Internet games are also starting to appear, for example, Worlds Inc.'s "Worlds Chat" and Parker Brothers' "Monopoly."

To actually produce a computer game clearly takes effort, but the basic tools are available to anyone with technical knowledge, a PC, and imagination. Further, the Internet can be used for marketing and distribution of the game, as discussed in chapter 8. The opportunities are limited only by the imagination of the entrepreneur!

Internet games

Microprose (CIVNet)
http://www.microprose.com

Worlds Inc. (Worlds Chat)
http://www.worlds.net

Parker Brothers (Monopoly)
http://www.monopoly.com

Business tip:
Internet games — Tools of the trade

If you want to get started writing your own IBM PC-compatible, Internet-based, multiplayer games, or you want to do your own "feasibility check," all you need is the following:

Reference material:

Building Internet Applications with Visual Basic by Michael Marchuk. Indianapolis, IN: Que Corporation, 1995

Visual Basic Multimedia Adventure Set by Scott Jarol. Scottsdale, AZ: Coriolis Group Books, 1994

Computer:
IBM compatible 386, 33 Mhz
80 Mb hard drive
4 Mb RAM

Software:
Windows 3.1
Microsoft Visual Basic V3.0

---

c. File archive service

File archives provide items such as help text files, computer applications, software source codes, and images for downloading to your computer using FTP. The Internet provides a wealth of publicly accessible file archive sites for every conceivable type of computer system. Companies such as Chestnut and Walnut Creek capitalize on the popularity of well-known public file archives by publishing CD-ROMs that are compilations of files available from popular Internet sites.

File archives are a very popular feature of BBS and OSP systems. The wide selection of freeware, shareware software, and media (e.g., sound, music, and pictures) that is available for download is usually the main draw. Two other key characteristics that draw and hold users is the size of the archive and how well it is refreshed with the latest software files available. File archives specializing in adult content have developed and have proven particularly popular.

BBSs and OSPs that charge access fees for such services are usually able to do so because of the value they add by providing files to the customer that have been prescreened for any software viruses. BBSs and OSPs also provide the basic classification service which eases the user's job of determining what files to select. Additional features provided to the user to support downloading include special highlighting to indicate new files and detailed text descriptions for each file.

We find that it is far easier to find a specific file on a BBS than on the Internet. The Archie tool is helpful for Internet searches, but it can't approach the utility of a well-managed and organized BBS file archive. The entrepreneur considering this business opportunity should consider using one of the well-established bulletin board software packages. Bulletin board software excels at the management of file archives, having all the facilities necessary to support large, easy-to-use file archives for PC systems, and can be set up and connected to the Internet in quick order.

For the entrepreneur, file archives as a commercial Internet venture present a real opportunity. Some of the most popular sites on the Internet are serviced using the resources of educational institutions. The popular sites are heavily overloaded and many have placed limitations on access times and number of simultaneous users. As Internet usage continues to increase, it is only a matter of time before educational services start to reconsider the free-access policy. Consequently, there exists an opportunity for entrepreneurs to set up and maintain commercial file archive sites, offering a high quality of service for a fee.

Operating such a file archive service on the Internet requires setting up a computer site that is permanently connected to the Internet using one of the methods described in chapter 9. The Web, WAIS, FTP, Telnet, and Gopher all lend themselves to support this type of business.

Popular file archive sites accessible over the Internet

Executive PC BBS
telnet://bbs.execpc.com
http://www.execpc.com

SimTel Coast to Coast Software Repository
http://www.coast.net/SimTel

Stanford University
ftp://sumex-aim.stanford.edu

Software Creations
http://www.swcbbs.com/

Washington University
ftp://wuarchive.wustl.edu

d. Electronic mall

There are many forms of electronic, or virtual, malls. These malls essentially provide an organized structure to support on-line business catalogues or advertisements. Electronic malls are usually operated by an OSP, ISP, or BBS.

The electronic mall operates in much the same way as a regular mall, with the owners charging rent to resident businesses or *storefront* owners. Rent may be in the form of a flat rate

Large electronic malls

Global Shopping Network
http://www.gsn.com

Internet Shopping Network
http://shop.Internet.net

Downtown Anywhere
http://www.awa.com/

Mega Mall
http://infotique.lm.com/megamall.html

Access Market Square
http://www.icw.com/ams.html

iMall
http://www.imall.com

based on the amount of information maintained in the mall, may include flat-rate monthly charges, or may be based on a percentage of sales achieved through the mall. The rent charged is also often related to the number of customers that the mall owner can draw to the electronic mall location.

The benefits of an electronic mall to the storefront owners are the same as for a normal mall: someone takes care of the infrastructure, other mall stores draw customers who may pause to visit your business, and your business benefits from promotion of the mall itself, which may draw potential customers.

Electronic mall owners often use various promotion methods to ensure a steady stream of potential customers to the site. Such methods include direct mail campaigns, print advertising, trade shows, and free information or entertainment content at the mall. Some electronic malls provide follow-up services to help bring back previous mall visitors.

One example of a follow-up technique is that used by the Internet Shopping Network (ISN). All potential customers are required to register with the mall to help with the ordering process. During the registration process, the customer is asked if he or she wants to receive direct e-mail announcements of special events and sales at the ISN. Those who answer yes receive infrequent e-mail highlighting special deals on merchandise. Other electronic malls try to entice return visits by providing free information that is time sensitive, while others provide some form of entertainment such as contests for free merchandise.

For entrepreneurs, setting up an electronic mall requires establishing a permanent presence on the Internet with a Web server, described in chapter 9. It also requires that you have access to the necessary technical, artistic, and marketing skills and resources to set up, maintain, and promote the mall.

There currently are many electronic shopping malls on the Internet. The most popular type, and the only one worth considering for this type of business, is a Web-based electronic mall.

A variation of the electronic mall is the electronic publication broker — the on-line equivalent of a bookstore or newsstand. The purely digital nature of electronic publications lends itself to a streamlined sales and delivery mechanism; the deal can be transacted and product delivered immediately. As an entrepreneur, you might set up a computer system permanently connected to the Internet where electronic publications may be

The Home Shopping Network and the Internet

It is interesting to note that the Internet Shopping Network (ISN) is a fully owned subsidiary of the very successful Home Shopping Network, one of the world's largest cable television retailers, with sales of $1.2 billion in 1993. Internet business is clearly being taken seriously by major players. The ISN offers more than 25,000 products from over 600 major companies.

ordered using an electronic order form. As an enticement to the customer, the site could offer concise summaries with graphics relevant to the publication, similar to the information contained on the cover of a book. This service could be offered using the Web, Gopher, or WAIS.

Electronic publication broker

First Virtual InfoHaus
http://www.infohaus.com

e. Internet directories

In chapter 4, we drew attention to the current state of affairs when it came to on-line directories for Internet resources. There are clearly business opportunities in this area. Big industry players, such as America Online, and entrepreneurs alike are flocking to get a piece of the directory action. Some of the more popular directory services such as Yahoo and Lycos have gone from being "hobbies" to successful businesses.

On-line directory services have the potential to bring in revenue from advertising, directory search fees, and directory registration fees. The most popular directories use the Web, Gopher, or WAIS tools.

At the top end, setting up an on-line Internet directory service with a broad scope (e.g., providing a directory service for any and every Internet resource) generally involves establishing a computer system permanently connected to the Internet via a leased line. The computer system would consist of one or more locally interconnected, high-end computers running applications that gather and index resources on the Internet. At the low end, setting up a limited-scope directory service, such as a specialized business directory, can be done using the Web and a virtual site service.

f. Interactive services

1. Personal match service

The personal match service typically allows individuals to post descriptions and preferences that are readily available for all to see. Anyone who is interested can then post a reply to initiate a dialogue. There are many types of personal match services, ranging from matching individuals for sports such as tennis to romance-oriented boards for different- or same-sex couples.

Personal match services accessible over the Internet

Match.com (Electric Classifieds, Inc)
http://www.match.com/

This service has revenue potential from advertising or through fees charged to the users of the service. The personal match service is a popular BBS business that is now also available on the Internet via Web or Telnet tools.

As an entrepreneur, you could implement a personal match service using e-mail, Telnet, the Web, and Gopher. For example, this service could be operated like an electronic personals listing using an e-mail mailing list and delivered using a dial-up computer running readily available e-mail software.

Alternatively, you could set up a computer system permanently connected to the Internet (the Web is the ideal tool for this one) that provides a set of "electronic want ad" categories, similar to newspaper classifieds. The site would allow customers to electronically type or load in information or graphics showing their item. The service would allow readers to select their items of interest from the categories and generate a response to the person placing the ad. You might charge by the length of the ad, frequency of the ad insertion, or by any other technique used by newspapers for such services.

These scenarios are just two ideas: many approaches are possible.

2. Conferencing services

There are various types of conferencing services in the on-line world of BBSs and OSPs that can be readily adapted to the Internet. In general, conferencing allows multiple individuals to discuss topics or otherwise interact. Participants type in their comments and submit them to the discussion group. All participants are presented with a simple scrolling text of all the submitted comments. Conferences may be oriented toward a specific topic or may be a free-for-all. Such conference services are also referred to as *chat services*.

Internet services such as this can be offered (and are being offered) using Web, Telnet, and custom software tools. The opportunity exists to extend this type of entertainment service using video conferencing technology or the multimedia capabilities of existing Internet tools.

Global celebrity interviews

Large OSPs periodically offer on-line conferences with celebrities. Celebrities interact with their electronic audience through an exchange of electronic messages. The audience can see the question posted to the guest by a member of the electronic audience or interviewer and then the response from the celebrity. This type of service has also been offered on an experimental basis on the Internet and has generated significant interest.

g. Selling advertising 🖥

In order for advertising to be effective on the Internet, it needs to be associated with a specific location where people gather. Many of the services previously discussed, and in particular, Internet resource directories or listing services, file archives, electronic magazines, e-mail discussion groups, and information services, may derive revenue from advertising. Once an Internet site is well established with hard statistics on the number of potential customers that visit, there is a basis for securing revenue from advertising.

There is also the potential for individuals to set up a business as a broker for advertising locations on the Internet, matching advertisers with Internet locations consistent with their market demographic and budget.

h. Paid Usenet participant 🖥

In many Usenet newsgroups, participants offer opinions on products and services. While overt advertising is not appropriate in many newsgroups, participant feedback is usually well received. Enterprising individuals are offering their services to business sponsors. These entrepreneurs will actively look for opportunities on Usenet newsgroups to represent a particular product in on-line discussions.

The paid Usenet participant may assume many different roles. You might monitor newsgroups relevant to the business you are representing and scan articles or postings, such as competitive information or customer queries and comments. Or you might respond to any questions or comments that you come across relating to the product or service, within guidelines agreed on by your sponsoring business.

Another role you might assume is that of reviewer, posting reviews and comparisons to relevant forums as a service to the Internet community. As long as you clearly identify yourself and the business you are representing, and your comparison is both objective and factual, your posting should be welcome. (See chapter 8 for a discussion on Usenet and advertising — what to do, and what not to do.)

Advertising space directories

Online Advertising Index
http://www.netcreations.com/ipa/ adindex/index.html

Traffic Resource
http://www.trafficresource.com/

i. E-mail services 🖥 to 🖥🖥🖥🖥

1. Electronic mailbox 🖥🖥🖥🖥

Electronic post office mailboxes

MyMail
http://www.mymail.com/

Pobox
http://www.pobox.com/

Internet users will want to find the best buy when it comes to ISPs, since rates and quality can vary widely. However, every time you change service providers, your e-mail address changes, unless you have your own domain name (as discussed in chapter 4).

A service that eliminates the e-mail address as a barrier to shopping around is an electronic post office mailbox. This service provides you with an e-mail address that remains constant regardless of which ISP you move to. All mail that arrives at the electronic post office mailbox is automatically forwarded to you at your current ISP e-mail address.

Running such a service involves setting up a computer system and software on the Internet that provides a mail account for customers for a nominal fee.

2. Anonymous re-mailer 🖥🖥🖥

Anonymous re-mailers

Community Connexion
http://www.c2.org

Anonymous re-mailer FAQ
http://www.well.com/user/abacard/ remail.html

For some interactions on the Internet, you may prefer to remain anonymous but reachable by e-mail (e.g., if you are responding to personal ads). Using an anonymous re-mailer service, the user (e.g., the person responding to a personal ad) sends a message to a particular intermediate computer system. This message has the address of its true destination embedded in its body. The intermediate computer takes the e-mail message and forwards it to its intended destination, substituting an anonymous address for the user's real e-mail address. The mapping between the user's real e-mail address and the anonymous address is maintained by the intermediate computer.

When e-mail is sent back to the user at the anonymous address, the intermediate computer receives the e-mail and forwards it to the real address, keeping the user's address hidden from the sender. When the user deletes his or her anonymous identification, no one is able to send any further e-mail to that user using the anonymous identifier. There are a number of popular informal services offering this service today.

For you to offer this service you will need computer system administration skills to set up and administer an out-of-the-box computer system, as well as set up and manage the appropriate software applications.

3. E-mail to post office letter

For businesses that use e-mail, there are services on the Internet that will convert e-mail directly into a post office letter without any more effort for you than normal e-mail takes to prepare and send.

As an entrepreneur, you could set up an e-mail address where people could submit their e-mail to be converted to traditional land mail. This is the electronic equivalent of the old-style telegram. Even in an electronic world, people still like to receive paper mail.

E-mail to U.S. post office

Outpost Network
http://www.outpost.net/

4. E-mail to pager service

E-mail can be readily integrated with other electronic communication services such as pagers. Such a service, created by taking existing software and hardware and "gluing" them together to create this capability, would be attractive to customers who already heavily rely on pagers. For instance, a realty agent who happens to use e-mail to interact with customers and potential buyers might want to be alerted when any e-mail arrives that indicates an interest in a specific property.

To operate such a system, you will need to set up a computer system permanently connected to the Internet, and then write software that will convert incoming e-mail to the appropriate pager message and then deliver that message to the customer's pager service.

E-mail to pager services

E-Page Systems
mailto:info@epage.com

Interpage Network Services
http://interpage.net/

Net Pager!
http://www.netpager.net/

5. Junk e-mail filter service

A service that filters e-mail for specific computer systems or individuals might be attractive to Internet users who have concerns regarding potential junk e-mail. The service would review all incoming e-mail and automatically delete e-mail that originates from specific people or Internet domains. Such a service is the equivalent of calling-number blocking that is available from some telephone companies (i.e., it lets you prevent unwanted individuals from tying up your telephone line or otherwise annoying you).

E-mail filtering service

Virtual E-mail
http://www.thebook.com/
mailto:info@thebook.com

As an entrepreneur, you could provide this service as part of an ISP service offering or as part of an electronic mailbox service, as described in this chapter. You would need to develop software to perform the filtering for specific e-mail accounts and either provide a master e-mail blocking list or provide the ability for individual customers to customize their filter.

6. Voice mail to e-mail conversion service

For those whose business operations are heavily integrated with e-mail, the ability for callers to generate e-mail messages rather than verbal messages is attractive. A voice mail to e-mail conversion service replaces the typical telephone answering machine or voice-mail service.

There are several ways in which the service can be realized using existing technology and software. The entrepreneur would act as system integrator, bringing together off-the-shelf equipment and either buying or writing the necessary software to glue it together. Once the system is ready, the entrepreneur might either sell prepackaged, shrink-wrapped setups, or sell and install the setups on a custom basis.

Both software and hardware are available that allow you to turn a computer into a voice answering machine capable of servicing multiple users. You might present callers with the choice of a fixed set of messages from which to select, in much the same way as they would with message services for pagers and cellular telephones. An alternative approach is to record, digitize, and compress the caller's voice message and package it into an e-mail message that can be heard through the recipient's computer. In both cases, calling-line identifier hardware, commonly available for PCs, can be readily integrated into the computer system to allow the originating telephone number to be automatically added to the e-mail message.

7. Office e-mail system interconnection

There are many proprietary office mail systems existing today. Multisite companies may choose a different e-mail package for each different office location. These represent islands, where users can communicate only within their local offices, or with other businesses that use similar software and for which they have set up special gateways that allow the businesses to exchange mail. Internet can be used as a means to "glue" together such islands. Almost every major office mail system (e.g., cc:Mail, MS-Mail) supports the ability to send and receive e-mail from the Internet.

Not every business has the expertise or understanding necessary to connect its systems to the Internet. For the technically proficient entrepreneur, there is an opportunity to step in and provide the integration expertise.

8. E-mailing list broker

While many Internet users do not want to receive unsolicited advertising, there are those who do desire specific items. Outside of the on-line world, it is not uncommon for customers to sign up for a business mailing list for catalogues or fliers. It is reasonable to expect that e-mailing lists will function in much the same way as traditional mailing lists, in terms of how they are collected and sold.

To take advantage of this opportunity, you might consider setting up a Web site where people can register to receive product e-mailings on a certain subject. An on-line instrument that provides categories of information that the users may freely subscribe to is the best way to create hassle-free Internet mailing lists. You might also charge advertisers for putting their products or services on the information posting board that is located at a heavily visited Internet address. A fee could then be charged to advertisers for the current mailing lists and ongoing updates. Naturally, if users want to get off a particular mailing list, they should have a mechanism for doing so. The best e-mailing list, and the only one that will protect the mailing list user from negative backlash, is one where all the e-mailing list members are added by request only and have been prevalidated in some way.

9. Mailing list service

Chapter 3 describes a popular use of e-mail for discussion groups, but e-mail discussion groups also have other potential commercial applications. One such application is as a service that offers private e-mail discussion groups for business or personal use. Such a service might be attractive to electronically inclined families or groups of friends who wish to keep in

Mailing list service

Mail Call
mailto:mailcall-info@mailcall.com

Spenser-Davis Group
http://www.spenser-davis.com/

touch. It's not uncommon today for family members to have access to e-mail from their home, office, or school computer.

A mailing list service gives a group its own mailing list, which allows members to keep in touch without having to remember a long list of Internet addresses. To deliver a message to all members of the group, members simply need to send their message to the single e-mail address of the e-mail discussion group. The service will then forward the message to all members. Members of the group may change their e-mail address registered with the mailing list as required so that they may remain in touch with a minimum of effort.

To run such a service requires knowledge of how to set up and manage an out-of-the-box computer system, as well as the associated data communications equipment and software applications.

10. Receiving e-mail by fax

Some businesses or individuals may want to receive e-mail from electronically connected customers, but don't want to originate or otherwise use e-mail. As an entrepreneur, you could set up a computer system that provides "read-only" e-mail accounts for users. All mail directed to the "read-only" e-mail addresses would be immediately forwarded directly to a fax machine specified by the user at the time of his or her subscription.

For example, a business might advertise an e-mail address to which orders may be sent. All orders would be printed out at the fax machine of the business.

This service may be useful to businesses such as fast-food delivery services that want to be accessible to local Internet customers without any Internet overhead other than waiting for e-mail faxes to arrive along with other normal fax orders.

11. E-mail faxing services

Faxes are an important business tool, and the value of integrating e-mail with faxes has been recognized on the Internet. Today, there are informal and commercial services available that convert and deliver e-mail to fax machines.

The services vary in terms of options and fee schedules. At the simplest level, the user sends an e-mail address to the service provider, indicating the destination fax number in the subject or body of the message. The service provider then converts the e-mail message to a fax and delivers the message as requested.

For business users, some services offer the option of translating the e-mail message body into a formal letter (including business letterhead or logos) to give a very professional-looking fax.

Internet e-mail-to-fax services may also be used to simplify distribution of faxes to multiple recipients by reducing the amount of time a user has to spend sending a fax. The option to have a return e-mail message confirming successful delivery of the fax to its intended destination is usually available.

As an entrepreneur providing this service, you will need to set up a computer system that is permanently connected to the Internet, write software to receive incoming e-mail messages, determine mapping to fax numbers, and initiate a fax modem software application to dial up and send the messages to the associated fax machine.

12. Moderated discussion groups

There is great potential for a business to set up with the sole purpose of managing an e-mail discussion mailing list. Usenet and unmoderated mailing list discussions can sometimes be low quality because of the number of off-topic messages that exist. For the entrepreneur moderating, two sources of income are possible: first, from sponsors who pay a fee to have their names and one or two lines of advertising appear somewhere in all mailing list messages sent out to subscribers, and, second, from voluntary or mandatory subscription fees from all mailing-list participants.

j. Fax on demand

Many companies today make use of automated fax-on-demand delivery systems. These systems allow a customer to use a touch-tone telephone to select from a range of product information documents. After making the document selection, users key in their fax numbers. The fax delivery system will send the requested document to them.

E-mail faxing services

AnyWare Associates FAXiNET
http://www.awa.com/faxinet/

Interpage Network Services
http://interpage.net/

Moderated discussion groups

Internet Marketing
http://www.popco.com/hyper/internet-marketing

Fax on demand

Ibex
http://www.ibex.com/

Any document imaginable can be converted into a fax — including troubleshooting tips, product specifications, and special coupons — and made available using this system. As a service, fax on demand can be readily integrated with the Internet, allowing customers to review and order documents using the Web, Telnet, or e-mail.

For businesses that already make use of such a system, integrating with the Internet can increase the flexibility and reach of the service. Fax can be an effective mechanism to deliver information with graphics to customers who are not able to access and view such documents on their computer. Integrating such a system with the Internet can also reduce overhead for your business by allowing you to have existing material simply scanned into a fax document database in order to make it available to Internet users.

To provide this service, you will need to set up one or more computers permanently connected to the Internet. There are various methods that may be used to implement this service. For the do-it-yourself entrepreneur, fax on demand may involve writing CGI scripts or software to link together commercial database and data communications software packages. Scripts and software may be required to manage a database program that will store the fax material. Special "glue" software may also be required to manage the data communications program that will deliver specific faxes to the customer's fax machine. For those who prefer the ready-made approach, there are commercial software packages available that already support this capability.

k. Internet training

Internet training for business customers is emerging as a small cottage industry. Training services that are emerging include one-on-one personal tutoring on software tools, seminar-based sessions, classroom training sessions, and self-directed computer-based training packages. As the Internet continues to grow in terms of its application and penetration into business and consumer markets, the demand for training related to the Internet and business applications is expected to continue.

For businesses looking for ways to upgrade the skills of their employees, on-line, self-paced training courses can be very economical. For businesses that currently specialize in training, the Internet provides an inexpensive vehicle to offer, or deliver, remote courses. Remote training of this nature is often referred to as distance learning. There are several companies operating on the Internet that specialize in on-line distance learning.

As an entrepreneur, you could program your own Web-based training courses and make them available remotely, using a virtual site service. You could also use the portable document format (PDF) (see section k in chapter 6) to package courses that are based primarily on traditional written materials to make the document available to any customer, regardless of the type of computer system they are using. In this case, you could deliver the resulting training files to customers using the FTP or e-mail tools.

On-line training courses

City University
http://www.cityu.edu/inroads/
welcome.html
mailto:info@cityu.edu

The New School
http://dialnsa.edu/home.html
mailto:info@dialnsa.edu

Walden University
http://www.waldenu.edu
mailto:request@waldenu.edu

l. Virtual businesses 💻💻💻

Virtual businesses are generating increasing interest as market and competitive pressures mount. Virtual businesses are composed of professionals who come together temporarily to collaborate on a contract. A key feature of this amalgamation is that the participants may be physically located in different cities and may work from home. For the entrepreneur, there exists the opportunity to offer custom Internet service packages that support the formation and operation of such virtual enterprises.

Virtual business service

Global Entrepreneurs Network
http://www.entrepreneurs. net/

The Internet provides an infrastructure to support a virtual business, particularly one that is knowledge based and doesn't require any physical office space or specialized equipment. The members of a virtual business collaborate on contracts, using e-mail to communicate and coordinate. To provide an external facade, all members of the business ideally need to have a common Internet business address (domain name). The desktop video conferencing capabilities supported by Internet applications are an effective alternative to traveling for business meetings.

Other Internet facilities associated with the domain name, such as Web and FTP sites, are also useful for sharing information and working with customers. Virtual business enterprises can also provide an on-line database of contacts and associated skills. Such a database would facilitate the formation of ad hoc teams.

Clearly, this opportunity is playing into the vision of the information-based society. You might put together a package of software and Internet services that would bundle video conferencing, FTP facilities, word processing, group scheduling, contact database management, collaborative tools (e.g., computer whiteboarding applications), e-mail services, a virtual Web server (see chapter 9), and relevant information databases. To support a full suite of services, you would need to set up and maintain a computer system permanently connected to the Internet.

m. Internet tool software

Internet tool software is a tremendous growth area. To the entrepreneur, the opportunities to set up shop are very attractive. Internet users are accustomed to electronic distribution and sales of software, so there is no barrier in that respect. The opportunities for software development are limited only by one's ability to identify a niche or need and hit the market faster than the next person.

Internet software applications can be developed by anyone with a computer and readily available software development tools. Moreover, the existence of industry-standard programming interfaces to the Internet — well-defined methods of writing a computer application so that the application, usually specific to a particular type of computer and operating system, can communicate with other applications that use the Internet — is making it easier to develop portable applications.

n. Internet demographic and statistics information service

To use the Internet effectively, businesses need reliable information on the use of specific services, customer traffic through specific Internet sites, and customer demographics. As it stands now, Internet demographics and statistical analysis are in their infancy. This area has caught the attention of companies such as Nielsen Media Research, a company well known for its work in analysis of television-related statistics. Nielsen has recently announced its intention to become more active in the analysis of the Internet.

Many entrepreneurs are currently making business out of available statistics, as well as generating their own through survey instruments placed on-line. The opportunity exists for you to apply traditional surveying techniques. Reliable demographic and statistical information will be of interest to the Internet business wishing to better understand the market and the opportunities available to it.

There is also an opportunity for you to provide specialized software and services to support the accurate measurement of customer visits to Internet resources, as is being done by I/PRO.

Internet demographic and statistics information services

Nielsen Media Research
http://www.nielsenmedia.com/

I/PRO Internet Profiler Corporation
http://www.ipro.com/

ActivMedia
http://www.activmedia.com

o. Internet business host or virtual site service

Not every business wants to set up and maintain its own computer system in order to have a 24-hour business presence on the Internet. The resulting business opportunity involves the setup and management of a pool of computers that provides a platform for other businesses to offer Internet applications and services such as Gopher sites, Web pages, e-mail info-servers, and Telnet-based catalogues.

To provide a virtual site service, you would need to set up one or more computers permanently connected to the Internet. The basic functionality required to support virtual sites is readily available on most Unix-based computer systems, but you will need a detailed understanding of computer system administration.

Internet business host service

Internet Business Solutions
http://www.inetbiz.com

p. Electronic cash services

While electronic cash services currently exist on the Internet, it is not immediately clear what direction such services are likely to go. While the natural way to make purchases over the Internet is using a credit card, there is concern over the security of these transactions. In response to these concerns, several Internet businesses offer an electronic cash service. These services are implemented using a variety of tools, but usually rely heavily on e-mail and Web tools.

The entrepreneurial "banker" might consider setting up a similar or competing service. This would involve developing specialized processes and software applications that would provide a secure mechanism to support financial transactions between both the customer and the vendor.

Electronic cash services

Cybercash
http://www.cybercash.com/

Digicash
http://www.digicash.com/

First Virtual
http://www.fv.com/

q. Internet marketing consultancy 🖥

Internet marketing consultancy is perhaps the biggest growth industry related to the Internet! The Internet has several mechanisms for publicizing your business, as described in detail in chapter 8. Opportunities lie in providing an Internet advertising strategy and implementation service to Internet-based businesses. This could be as simple as helping a business determine the appropriate Internet mechanisms for contacting customers or as detailed as actually implementing an agreed-on advertising strategy.

For a fee, this service could provide consultations on how best a business can publicize new Internet resources, analyze competitors' sites, and actively promote the Internet business. A good consultant can make operating on the Internet as straightforward to a businessperson as taking out an ad in a newspaper.

This specialized activity requires an intimate knowledge of the Internet, as well as associated information-searching tools and directories.

r. Internet authoring 🖥

Most businesses will not want to get involved in the technical details associated with setting up an electronic storefront and will look for experts who can provide the service in a cost-effective and timely fashion with some guarantee of delivering a professional product. Consequently, there is an opportunity to provide authoring services for Gopher menus, Web pages, canned content for mail responders, on-line electronic catalogues, and specialized off-line catalogue or advertising applications.

Web-page authoring is the most demanding authoring service and generally requires detailed technical, artistic, and journalistic knowledge. Web page preparation typically involves translating existing material provided by the customer into a suitable Web format. Authoring for Web pages that have a heavy graphic-design content requires specialized hardware to support converting photos and artwork to an electronic format.

However, many PC-based tools are currently available that allow very impressive Web page-based electronic catalogues to be authored in a manner much like any other computer drawing package. The technical expertise required to support Internet authoring is expected to decline with the increasing availability of these design-assist tools.

s. Internet security services

The security concerns identified in chapter 5 present business opportunities for computer experts versed in security technologies. Configuring, installing, and testing Internet security systems will be in demand.

As an entrepreneur, you may choose to set up shop as a security planning consultant, security system integrator, or security problem troubleshooter/investigator. In order to be successful, you will need an intimate knowledge of Internet security issues and practices. A knowledge of specific hardware and software security products may be necessary. A detailed knowledge of one or more specific computer and operating systems and associated security details would be beneficial.

t. Internet service provider (ISP)

Providing customers with Internet access such as SLIP/PPP and shell access (as discussed in chapter 2) appears to be one of the largest growth opportunities associated with the Internet today. The initial capital costs are low, as are incremental growth costs. The barrier is primarily a technological one, since the setup and administration of a profitable ISP require skilled staff. Poor skill and lack of discipline can have a serious impact on customer satisfaction. We personally left our first ISP because helpline support was poor and the Internet access provided was irregular and undependable.

Turn-key ISP vendor

CERAM
(Internet starter kit)
http://www.ceram.com/

Celestial Systems, Inc.
http://www.celestial.com

> ### Business tip:
> ### How to get started as an Internet service provider
>
> If you are considering starting up your own business to offer Internet access, a good place to begin is with the *Internet Access Provider FAQ* by David H. Dennis. This FAQ provides information on everything you need to know to put together a business case and set up your business. The FAQ includes practical information from a number of entrepreneurs already operating their own ISP businesses. The FAQ is available free of charge on the Internet at *http://www.amazing.com/*.
>
> Another relevant FAQ that is specifically geared to inexpensive PC setups (e.g., 386 PCs) using the Linux operating system as the basis for offering Internet access, is available at: *http://www.anime.net/linuxisp/Linux-ISP-HowTo.html*.

u. Family-oriented Internet service

Internet is not the sort of playground in which you would want to let your children roam free. The Internet is like any community, having both a good side and a dark side. The Internet has adult material readily available in Usenet newsgroups, file archive sites, chat conferences, and Web sites.

The availability of such material presents the opportunity to set up and run a family-oriented Internet access service. Such a service blocks access to Internet resources or sites that are known to contain adult content. The potential demand for such a service is evidenced by the existence of several PC-based programs that screen Internet access from the home.

A centralized screening solution that is part of an ISP's basic Internet access package may be more attractive to parents than the PC-based programs, which have overhead associated with keeping the screening capabilities up to date. As well, the PC-based programs also have the potential to be circumvented by intelligent young minds.

A centralized ISP-based service may be implemented using any number of approaches. The best approach might be to provide regularly updated and validated screening facilities that allow access to specific Internet resources that have been prescreened and approved as "family oriented."

v. Technical support and consulting

Internet is inherently computer based. Consequently, any existing computer consulting company is well positioned to provide the necessary support to customers to set up and manage Internet applications.

This opportunity would require trained staff who are knowledgeable in computers and the range of Internet applications that can be set up on them. Your business would operate like a professional services organization that charges a fee or sets up a flat-rate contract for services over a specified period of time. Many other creative opportunities exist where customer knowledge is low and there is a real technical need to be filled.

w. Publications and periodicals

There are over 200 Internet-related books currently in print, ranging from general "how to" books to specialized technology-oriented books. There has also been a growth in Internet periodicals, newsletters, and journals. Considering the rapid advances in technology and techniques, the demand for current information related to the Internet is expected to continue unabated.

The entrepreneur with practical how-to knowledge or detailed technical knowledge, coupled with strong technical writing skills, is well positioned to self publish, broker other technical organizations' publications, or freelance. The electronic publication capabilities on the Internet mean that you have alternative methods to publish outside of traditional print media.

Note: We don't have any recommendations for which route you should take: self publishing or approaching established publishers. Both routes can lead to success.

x. Language translation service 🖥

The Internet consumer and business community encompasses many different languages; English is definitely not the only language used. Companies wanting to undertake business internationally will be faced with the need for translation services at one time or another, unless they have the skills in-house. For companies wishing to do business globally, language translation will apply not only to e-mail correspondence but also to the business's Web and Gopher information services. There are numerous human-based translation services available on the Internet.

The Internet presents the potential of increased demand for translation services, as well as providing a mechanism for existing translation services to extend the reach of their business.

Language translation services

AAArt Web Design
http://www.catalog.com/aaart/

Aleph —
The Global Translation Alliance
http://www.aleph.com/

China Hangzhou Hope
Translation Co. Ltd
http://chinapages.com/Interpreters/

Language Engineering Corporation
http://www.lec.com/

y. CD-ROM publishing 🖥

The Internet contains a great pool of public information, although it is not always well organized. Opportunities exist for the entrepreneur to organize and publish this information using CD-ROMs. A number of companies have already recognized this and have published CD-ROM collections of information gleaned from the Internet. CD-ROM content ranges from complete copies of popular Internet file archive sites to collected freeware and shareware games.

The technology to create a CD-ROM template for manufacture is readily available. For example, Corel sells a software package that assists you in preparing a master CD-ROM. A manufacturer can then replicate thousands of copies from the CD-ROM master for approximately $1.40 or less per CD-ROM.

CD-ROM publishing

InfoMagic
http://www.infomagic.com

Walnut Creek
http://www.cdrom.com
ftp://ftp.cdrom.com

Microforum
http://www.microforum.com

Corel Corporation
http://www.corel.com

Corel Corporation
1-800-394-3729
Software: Corel CD Creator

KAO Infosystems
1-800-759-2590
Service: CD-ROM replication and associated services

8.

Operating an Internet business

Is there such a thing as an Internet sales call? What kind of business system should you establish to attract customers, get them to purchase your product, and provide service to them after the initial purchase? How can you present a professional image to potential customers at your Internet site? Which of the many Internet tools should you use to present your corporate image to the outside world?

The majority of businesses today are using the Internet to let the world know about their company and the kinds of products or services they provide, as well as to improve their internal and external communications infrastructure. To attract potential customers to their Internet site, many companies are currently advertising their e-mail, FTP, or Web addresses both on-line and through traditional paper-based advertisements, using business cards, correspondence material, and paper-based marketing material, printed advertising in magazines and newsletters, and Internet directories or Usenet newsgroups.

Today, only a small percentage of businesses are performing sales transactions over the Internet. This is because most companies do not have a detailed understanding of how to best use Internet technology to meet their overall corporate goals. Most businesses, however, believe that they will eventually be able to conduct at least part of their sales transactions on-line. Creating a corporate strategy that allows your company to extend

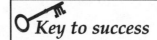

Key to success

Develop a unified Internet market strategy
If you have multiple business offices, you should develop a unified strategy for use of the Internet, and specifically the Web, before you spend any money. In particular, ensure that only one office or department is responsible for implementing your external business presence on the Internet. The global nature of the Internet removes the need for regional implementations.

its Internet presence to perform on-line sales transactions is a logical step to improving your bottom line.

In this chapter, we examine the various approaches to creating, advertising, marketing, and operating your Internet presence on a daily basis. Presenting a good corporate image on the Internet using the various tools is discussed, though we concentrate on the use of the Web, e-mail, and newsgroups as the primary tools for business. Remember, it is important when implementing your Internet presence to know what tools your customers are using, as this will affect the tools you use. You may want to review chapter 1 to reconfirm who your customers are and how they are accessing the Internet. Creating Web sites that will keep your customers coming back is also discussed.

In addition, this chapter looks at methods to handle sales or informational transactions, should you decide that you want to move some of your sales effort on-line.

a. Six steps to operating your business

Every seasoned sales and marketing organization knows by heart the six cardinal steps in marketing and selling its product or service:

(a) Prospect for new customers.

(b) Qualify leads by determining customer interest and ability to pay.

(c) Present the product sales pitch.

(d) Handle objections.

(e) Close and process the sale.

(f) Handle after-sales service.

How should you apply these well-known principles to your Internet business? The Internet on-line sales business dynamic has a number of characteristics that complicate some aspects of the sales process but that also make other parts easy. You will need to understand this dynamic as you develop the operations, technology, and organizational infrastructure to support this new environment. A good business process will take into account the Internet's sales and marketing "environment" conditions surrounding the merchant and customer:

- On-line business is a faceless transaction between you and the customer (a similar situation to catalogue shopping).

- The customer base is global and culturally varied.

- Customers find your site through advertising, word-of-mouth, or accidentally.

- Customers may come day or night (inside or outside of your regular business hours).

- Customers will need a great deal of information to make a decision to buy (since they aren't standing in front of the product or salesperson).

- Customers will be concerned with your reliability as a vendor (since they likely haven't dealt with you before).

- Establishing interpersonal relationships will be difficult but not impossible.

- Handling objections to purchasing your product or service will be difficult since it is a faceless transaction.

- Customers may want various methods to purchase the product, since there is concern about passing credit card information over the Internet.

- Surveying and obtaining feedback from your customers will be easy.

- Collecting data on your sales process will be easy.

- Competitors can access your site as easily as customers.

If you examine the characteristics of the above sales and marketing dynamic, you can in effect compress the sales pro-cess to fit the Internet environment. There are four main steps that you must organize your business around. You will need to —

(a) prospect electronically or through traditional means for new customers,

(b) electronically present your product sales pitch and handle objections automatically through your electronic sales outlet presentation (best handled through a Web site presence),

(c) electronically or manually close and process the sale, and

(d) electronically or manually handle after-sales service.

The remainder of this chapter is dedicated to describing the approaches you need to use to implement a successful business presence and on-line sales and marketing strategy.

b. Electronic prospecting on the Internet

"There's gold in them thar networks." How much gold you get depends on how well you structure your Internet-based advertising and marketing strategy. Physical location of the business in an electronic environment is not the determining factor; rather, it is more a matter of leaving trails of electronic bread crumbs leading to your business site around the network. Creating electronic links from many other sites to your site will allow customers to beat a path to your door.

1. Traditional methods

There are many tried-and-true methods of prospecting in the nonInternet world. Seasoned sales and marketing teams will recognize these techniques and be able to apply many of them to support an Internet-based business environment.

(a) **Advertising:** Buy a small piece of advertising space in a magazine, periodical, newspaper, radio, or television spot to sell your product or service and receive customer enquiries.

Applicability to the Internet: Advertising is a good fit to the Internet. Advertise in Internet-specific magazines and on the Internet through mall operators, ISPs, OSPs, and BBSs to take advantage of their built-in facilities for passive advertising.

(b) **Informal leads through nonbusiness organizations:** Some of the best business contacts are made through service organizations, professional groups, clubs, or associations.

Applicability to the Internet: Obtaining informal leads will involve some interpersonal "schmoozing" with your prospective customers through Usenet discussion groups.

(c) **Leads through satisfied customers:** Happy customers are always willing to recommend you to new customers if they trust your company and service.

Applicability to the Internet: Such leads are a good fit to the Internet. The customer can forward a favorable e-mail message or your site name with a simple point-and-click!

(d) **Active canvassing:** Call your prospects on the telephone or go door to door to try to get them to donate to a cause or buy your product.

Applicability to the Internet: You can canvas actively in newsgroups, or through direct e-mail, but be warned — you may get negative reaction, possibly resulting in your business being denied Internet access.

(e) **Contests:** Everyone likes to win a contest and by entering your contest, potential customers provide you with their names and addresses which you may wish to add to your mailing list.

Applicability to the Internet: Contests are a great idea! Internet users generally like electronic games, so you may have a lot of fun getting your next wave of customers this way.

(f) **Directories and mailing lists:** You can buy mailing lists for almost any specific demographic group you want; most magazines sell their mailing lists.

Applicability to the Internet: Fits like a glove — e-mail mailing lists are the electronic equivalent of the paper world. In addition, you have many demographic groups already organized around discussion groups. Register yourself in the various informal directories on the Internet.

(g) **Group plans:** Cater to groups or give corporate discounts on products if there are enough participants.

Applicability to the Internet: Group plans may be a very good approach if you are trying to sell to corporations or nonprofit organizations.

(h) **Information exchanges:** Salespeople from companies that aren't in competition with yours might be willing to exchange useful information with you.

Applicability to the Internet: Information exchanges have possibilities through on-line forums such as Usenet newsgroups.

(i) **Internal records:** If you are a medium- to large-sized company, you may have another organization within your firm that already has a list of possible Internet customers.

Applicability to the Internet: Sounds logical, but there will be no impact on the Internet business other than having another mailing list at your disposal.

(j) **Sales force and informal "opportunity spotters" observations:** This technique requires an observant salesperson or someone who is close to the customers to scan nontraditional sources of customer information such as death notices, divorces, and estate sales.

Applicability to the Internet: Internet-literate salespeople who know their way around the electronic environment can continually look for new sites to post electronic links to your site and business information.

(k) **Your service personnel:** Service people within your organization are a valuable link to your existing customers.

Applicability to the Internet: Use the customer and service personnel interaction mechanism to draw out new customers, using e-mail as your primary tool.

(l) **Trade shows:** Attend and participate in trade shows, and make contact with prospective customers for further business.

Applicability to the Internet: Why not? If you're at a trade show, make sure that your business cards or product information include your electronic site address.

(m) **Reader service and referral and warranty registration cards:** Magazines have cards in them that readers fill out to get more product information. These cards can turn into valuable leads.

Applicability to the Internet: Modernize these cards and put your electronic address on them! Put your information on-line.

(n) **Business guides:** Business guides include the names, addresses, and corporate information that may be used to gain new contacts.

Applicability to the Internet: Make sure your business's electronic address is in local, regional, national, and international business directories.

(o) **Government publications:** Government publications often include valuable demographic information that is otherwise difficult to get.

Applicability to the Internet: Some publications may exist in which you can publish your business's electronic address.

(p) **Indexes of published information:** Trade association directories are useful sources of information on potential customers.

Applicability to the Internet: You may consider sending trade associations your electronic address to encourage employees and subscribers to visit your site.

Business tip:
Keep your Internet address
memorable and portable!

There is significant advantage to having an easily remembered, short Internet address (a text address, as opposed to the numeric address). The longer and more obscure the Internet address, the more likely it is that your potential customers will make a mistake typing it when they try to connect to your electronic storefront. Also, any name that imparts some information about your business will work to your advantage if someone is simply looking at a list of URLs, deciding where to browse next.

Perhaps the most important consideration is to obtain for your business an Internet address that is portable between ISPs. During this period of rapid growth of businesses providing Internet access, access costs are certain to continue to decline. Owning a portable Internet address will give your business the freedom to move between ISPs without causing any major discontinuity for your customer base.

There are two ways to obtain a portable and easily remembered URL. The first, preferred way is to obtain your own domain name. Many ISPs will take care of the paperwork necessary to secure a suitable Internet address for you as part of your service contract or for a minimal annual charge of about $50 (after the initial setup fee of $100). The second way is to pay for an electronic post office box. This is a service provided by some businesses on the Internet where you are assigned a URL on a computer for a small yearly fee, about $10. You can then have mail redirected to whatever your current, "real" URL address is at your local ISP (see chapter 7 for more details).

If you want to register your own domain name, contact *http://www.internic.net/* for more information.

---

2. Nontraditional methods

A good prospecting method incorporates the traditional prospecting methods as well as taking into account experience gained from actual Internet use. Experience on the Internet has shown that most people find out about new sites primarily through one of four ways:

(a) Recommendations from their friends or associates

(b) Informally maintained Internet electronic or paper directories (available in bookstores)

(c) A magazine or journal

(d) Usenet newsgroups

One of the reasons users find out about sites in this ad hoc fashion is because of the lack of a centralized Internet directory service. A concise list of some of the more popular informal on-line directories is found in chapter 4.

You need to take into account how users find sites when planning your prospecting.

(a) Capitalize on Usenet newsgroups

The Usenet newsgroup tool is an ideal way of finding out who is interested in your particular product or service area. It is a general misconception that Usenet is off limits to business. However, before getting carried away trying to make use of newsgroups for commercial purposes, you should understand the term *netiquette*. Netiquette refers to the unwritten rules of acceptable behavior for the electronic community (primarily Usenet communities) in which you are attempting to provide product or service information. The golden rules, if you are to be successful in promoting your product or service, are to use good sense, not be overt in your advertisements, and only advertise in appropriate areas.

Be sure to read the newsgroup's FAQs to see whether that particular newsgroup allows advertising (in fact, there are some newsgroups whose primary purpose is advertisements), and do not advertise in those that explicitly exclude commercial activity. While Usenet is a tool that should not be ignored by your business, it is not a tool that you should use without research and consideration.

Some general guidelines to follow when posting to a newsgroup include the following:

---

*How users find out about Web pages ***

(Respondents answered more than one category, thereby causing percentages to be more than 100%.)

- From friends and other pages 95.71%
- From magazines 64.3%
- From Usenet 58.79%

Prodigy users:

- From Usenet 38%

GTRC 1995 Survey

(a) Don't post articles that are a personal attack on anyone.

(b) Make your postings clear, understandable, and appropriate to the newsgroup: off-topic advertisements are considered to be rude intrusions. Also remember that each message posted uses disk space at the user's end, and so irrelevant advertisements are not tolerated.

(c) Don't engage in lengthy discussions in the newsgroup if the topic is not likely to be of particular interest or relevance to the rest of the participants. If a discussion becomes lengthy, it is best to take the conversation off-line onto private e-mail between you and the other person.

How should you approach Usenet newsgroups in order to attract willing customers and avoid offending the community? The best way is to take a low-key friendly approach in which you are a contributing member of the discussion group or electronic community.

Business tip:
Don't spam!

Spamming is the posting of advertisements to inappropriate Usenet newsgroups, or the posting of off-topic messages to more than one newsgroup. Spamming is a bad business strategy for getting ahead on the Internet. It can generate a great deal of negative feeling toward you and your business, and will likely do your business more harm than good. By spamming, you could also be violating your acceptable-use agreement with your ISP, and might lose your Internet access as a consequence.

Spamming can draw the wrath of other Internet users in many forms, including hate e-mail and e-mail bombing attacks (where your e-mail account is inundated by several thousand e-mail messages).

If you plan to try to make use of the over 10,000 existing Usenet newsgroups, here are the salient points that will make your task easier and more profitable.

(a) **Participate in newsgroups of particular relevance:** The best way to approach using newsgroups as part of your business operation is to survey the lists of existing newsgroups and select those you feel might have potential interest in your product area. It is best to regularly participate in the ongoing discussions to build up your credibility and goodwill with the group. During this period you can spot opportunities in which you can present arguments in favor of products or services from your business. If you respond to comments from anyone, be sure to include your short e-mail signature (see chapter 3) which includes advertising for your business. Also be sure to be brief, concise, and accurate, since most people on the newsgroup don't want to receive longwinded e-mails that have little to contribute to the discussion at hand.

As well, independent of overt advertising you may gain from participating in noncommercial newsgroups, you may derive a better understanding of the needs of potential customers, or develop leads or contacts.

(b) **Provide selected announcements to well-matched newsgroups:** Once you have identified target newsgroups, you should prepare a short note containing specific and concisely written facts about your product or service, and post it to the newsgroup which may benefit from knowledge about your product or service. In your note, point interested parties to a Gopher, FTP, or Web site, or an e-mail address for more information. Remember, this announcement should be a short note, not a full-blown sales pitch.

(c) **Set up your own newsgroup on Usenet:** What a great idea! If there aren't any current newsgroups fitting your business's bill, why not set up and control your own? This is entirely feasible, but you will need to ensure that the discussion group has some value to it in order to attract and keep participants. Make sure users are getting useful information about the particular subject area on which you are focusing, as well as finding out about your product. If your newsgroup is completely commercial you will find cyberspace a very lonely place.

A word of caution before you get carried away with setting up your own newsgroup: technical expertise and maintenance are required to ensure that users are happy, that the information being exchanged is relevant, and that other companies aren't trying to crash your newsgroup party!

(d) **Avoid aggressive advertising approaches on Usenet:** If you are an aggressive advertising type, friendly and unobtrusive methods may seem slow in getting results, and you may want to get in fast and get the job done quickly. In this case, the option of posting your advertisements or solicitations on all Usenet groups is open to you. Don't be surprised, however, if you receive a lot of criticism mixed with some potential customer replies.

Also, you should be aware that automated facilities are in place at some sites that will attempt to delete your advertisement from the newsgroups earlier than normal. The use of this aggressive technique is relatively new to Usenet and may cause you grief and turn off your customer base before you've had a chance to work with them and build rapport. It would be well worth your time to first observe the lay of the land before trying to cross it. Remember, you may suffer denial of service because you violated an acceptable-use policy.

(b) Update informal Internet directories

There are many informal directories on the Web in which you can register your business address for free. The Yahoo site is the best known of these informal directory sites. It may take two weeks or more from the time you register to the time your site is listed and visible to the general Internet public. Refer to the list of directory locations found in chapter 4 in order to start populating your Internet site. Most directories provide self-explanatory directions on how to register.

Key to success

Announcing your Web site
The FAQ "How to announce your new web site" may be found at: *http://ep.com/faq/ webannounce.html.*

Business tip:
Experience in publicizing a Web-page location

Web directories are varied in their content, presentation of available directory entries, search methods, frequency of information update and validation, and the information screening and submission process. We wanted to publicize a Web site that provided references for aviation aficionados. We tried to get the Web site's URL entered into as many of the Internet informal and specialized directories as possible, but found that the processes and effort required for requesting URL-inclusion in the directories varied widely. The time taken to update a directory varied between next-day service and not getting updated at all. The effort to publicize the page amounted to over 12 hours of on-line effort to submit the requests and follow up to see if the URL had made it into the directory.

Some companies have recognized this update problem and have devised a method of simplifying a submission to many sites. Someone wanting to submit to many sites enters the request into a single site. The submission is then automatically registered with all the other sites. This technology eliminates the need to visit multiple sites.

(c) Create business relationships with other companies

As you work your way through the Internet, you will begin to notice that there are many Internet locations that appear to have some relation to your business. Nowhere is this more obvious than when using the Web. Many companies are creating partnerships where they each cross-post the other's site on their respective systems. This is a very clever approach but requires an observant sales and marketing person to be able to build the intercorporate relationships as well as spot opportunities.

Fortunately, all of this can be done on-line, and you don't have to leave your office to reap the benefits. If you decide to take this approach, you should recognize that you need to periodically survey these cross-posting sites to ensure that the information is accurate and that you haven't been accidentally erased from cyberspace!

If you are using the Web, you would ask the other company to create a hypertext link to your site. Once the customer presses the highlighted text on the other company's Web page, your site is located and automatically appears on the customer's computer screen. Gopher tools also allow for cross posting.

(d) Advertise at Internet on-ramps

Most users accessing the Internet must enter through an ISP, OSP, or BBS. In many cases, these operators provide a "welcome" screen, which supports advertising, when users first log on. Advertising in this way will likely cost you money, but there is good potential for getting your Internet site location and business message out.

(e) Use e-mailing lists

E-mailing lists are the electronic equivalent of direct mailing lists in the physical world. There are three main ways to build or obtain customer lists that would fit your product or service.

First, you could monitor newsgroups that are likely to attract people who would be interested in your product or service, and collect the mail addresses of participants to form an e-mailing list. This list could then be used for focused solicitation in much the same way as a normal mailing list is used for a mail order business. Remember, users on your list should agree to receive your updates before you start flooding them with advertisements.

Second, you could purchase an e-mailing list from a reputable broker and use this for direct customer solicitation.

The third, and recommended approach is to get customers to sign up to your mailing lists voluntarily. Tools such as Gopher, Telnet, and the Web are ideal for allowing users to sign up and maintain control over who is sending them material. You can also have users check a box on your reader service or warranty cards if they want further information sent to their e-mail address. Once you have the mailing list in your hands, you will need to think about how you will approach your customers. Include only relevant information about your product or service and where customers can get more information from your Internet location, and try to keep your e-mail short and to the point.

Note: Unsolicited e-mail advertising is not generally well received on the Internet and is not a recommended practice. Further, as with spamming, you could be violating the acceptable-use policy of your ISP and might lose your Internet access as a consequence.

(f) Use FTP and electronic infomercials

Using FTP and electronic infomercials is an alternative method of providing product details for the computer literate consumer. FTP is the tool of choice for this application. A potential customer retrieves a copy of a piece of software from your Internet FTP site; the software contains your infomercial ready to be viewed. Here's how the procedure works:

(a) Create an electronic infomercial and an executable program that customers can run on their computers (usually you compress the program first, so downloading the software doesn't take so long).

(b) Upload the infomercial to your advertised FTP site.

(c) Advertise the location of your infomercial in a clever way (perhaps through a contest).

(d) Customers download your infomercial, unpack the executable program, and play the infomercial describing your product or service on their computer.

Always remember that Internet users are constantly on the lookout for new, innovative, and clever ideas, so be sure to include something to satisfy this need in your infomercial.

(g) Alternative advertising techniques

There are other ways to get free publicity for your Internet site and business, in addition to the electronic techniques described above. Alternative advertising techniques you might try include the following:

(a) Contact paper directory publishers to list your site.

(b) Contact Internet consultants to list your site.

(c) Try to get some print magazines to review your site.

(d) See if you can get the local newspapers to review your site; they may be interested in your use of the Internet.

(e) Write a magazine article about your innovative site.

c. Creating a winning World Wide Web site

The single most popular form of Internet presence being used by companies today is the Web site. A successful Web site may incorporate graphics, audio, text, and e-mail, as well as allow for on-line sales transactions.

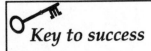

Key to success

Integrate with print advertising!

Put your Internet address on your business card and print ads. It is a simple method to let potential customers know where to get additional information or how to contact you. As an example, you might put:

http://StuffIsUs.WWW.biznet.com

mailto:StuffIsUs@biznet.com

Once you've managed to attract your prospective customers to your Web site, you will have to maintain their attention, create interest in your product, generate the desire and commitment to purchase your product, and motivate them to complete your electronic order form. Before customers purchase your product, nagging doubts may enter their minds as they ask themselves if the benefits of your product outweigh the cost. Unfortunately, you won't be there in person to handle their objections, so your electronic presence must attempt to do it for you.

There has been a great deal of literature written on customer psychology and selling, and how to present your product or service in a series of steps designed to break down the sales resistance of the customer. Most of these techniques involve subtle or not-so-subtle progressive stages of human interaction between the salesperson and the target customer.

In the Internet environment, customers can electronically appear and disappear in seconds. During those brief first few seconds or minutes when you have the customers' attention, you must capture their imagination and keep them on your site long enough to convince them to buy your product or service.

What, then, should your Internet presence collectively do? What are the visible and invisible messages that you should try to get across? How should you present your business image? How can you make it easy for your prospective customers to purchase your product or service?

Rather than trying to think of everything at once, break down the content of your site by using standard sales and marketing approaches to turn your site into an effective extension of your business. The major steps to a successful Internet site are the following:

(a) Present a professional corporate image.

(b) Make your site dynamic, interesting, and efficient to use.

(c) Establish your business and products' benefits to customers early in their visit.

(d) Anticipate your customers' questions.

(e) Provide a simple, secure ordering and billing procedure.

(f) Provide an active customer feedback mechanism so you can continually improve your site content and presentation.

(g) Allow for human contact for customers who need attention.

1. Present a professional corporate image

It is clear from survey feedback that on-line customers are concerned about the quality and reliability of on-line vendors. According to Georgia Tech Research Corporation survey results, 84% of users indicate that vendor reliability is a major issue, and 89% feel that the quality of information they obtain off the network is a major issue. In presenting a professional image, you must create a corporate image that projects reliability and quality to the community. This can be achieved by using the following techniques:

(a) Welcome your customers and present them with a small but attractive corporate logo.

(b) Provide a corporate profile that includes how many years you have been in business, and the location, size, and growth potential of your company. Use a similar approach to that used in the stock market to obtain investors through prospectus material, in order to develop confidence that your business is not going to fold tomorrow.

(c) Provide news releases or articles about your business's product or service so that customers can see how well known and dynamic you are in the industry.

(d) Ensure that material you are putting on your site is accurate. You should thoroughly research any material you present, and have an editing and fact-checking team check the accuracy of your material as a quality control process.

(e) Provide information that is both of interest to people and that is indirectly related to your products (e.g., position papers on technical subjects or commentary on various technologies).

(f) Demonstrate that you are a good Internet corporate citizen by showing customers that you are a participating member in various forums and that all your activities are not for profit alone. Just as many traditional businesses donate to charity or endowment funds, you may want to provide space for Web sites for nonprofit organizations if you have server space, or donate equipment or funds to community freenets in order to increase your on-line visibility and generate goodwill with Internet users. Another approach is to provide free information to the Internet user community on subjects of interest.

You may decide to create your own Web site or you may decide to use a supplier who specializes in Web site creation. If you choose to buy, you should be sure to test drive the final product. It is wise to go through an acceptance testing phase before paying the consulting company.

2. Make your site dynamic, interesting, and efficient to use

Make your site "cool" to appeal to the age of your average Internet user. You'll notice that many Internet users want to be on the leading edge of what's happening in the network and they are continually on the search for "hot" places to visit. Successful sites learn to adapt and cater to the culture of the Internet community. One of the best ways of gauging your site is to electronically visit your competitors' sites to see what they are up to and how they have approached their corporate image presentations.

One key quality of a good site is informative, useful, and regularly updated information. This can be maintained by providing a fast-loading index of the material in your site, as well as a "what's new" section that can be accessed directly by repeat visitors. Users should also be able to interact with your site and be entertained as much as possible, so that a more personal relationship between the user and your company develops.

Sites that seemingly take forever for users to load into their computer and display on their screens because of large graphics files or other reasons are a major source of irritation. Longwinded sites will be quickly passed over as users sit, fidget, and finally "time out," or give up, waiting for the long file transfers to complete. Even at the fast access speed of 28.8 Kbps (which is the access speed for a minority of users), graphically intensive Web pages are painful to wait for and use. We have disconnected from many commercial sites because of lengthy waiting time.

To maximize the usability of your Web site for customers, we recommend the following guidelines:

(a) If you are planning to include any large, embedded graphics or photos, provide an option to users of a text-only or graphics-rich interface on the first page. This way, your site can cater to all customers.

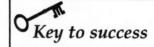

Key to success

Try before you buy!
It may seem like a silly thing to point out, but before you accept a set of Web pages prepared for your business by consultants or internal personnel, sit down and try them yourself, using a terminal connected to the Internet by a 28.8 Kbps modem. Look for two things:

(a) Does the finished product reflect what you want in terms of use and presentation? We have come across many Web sites that are completely unusable. The most common problem we encountered is too much graphical content, exceeding our willingness to wait for the browser to download and display it. Unintelligible text and graphics have also proved to be very annoying.

(b) Are all the features of the Web pages functional? For instance, we have come across business sites that were not working. We tried to submit an order for a magazine subscription and the site was non-functional!

(b) Provide small images of photos (referred to as *thumbnails*) that users may select if they want to view larger, more detailed photos. A large photo (5" x 4") may take upward of one minute to load using a 14.4 Kbps modem. Giving customers good prior knowledge about what they are about to download can avoid frustration and allow customers to determine how best to spend their on-line time visiting your Web site.

(c) Keep information content partitioned into related and stand-alone pages (preferably one to two PC screens at a time) to minimize the amount of scrolling users have to do once the page of information has arrived.

(d) Provide *hotlinks* at the bottom of each Web page to allow users to rapidly return to a top level Web page without having to hunt for it (which for some users involves the painful process of having to reload pages until they get back to where they want to be). This will help optimize customers' visit time by ensuring that it is spent browsing information and not waiting on the modem.

If you have a large catalogue or advertising content, you may want to consider other alternatives to maximize the value of your information to customers. An alternative to real-time on-line viewing is to package your Web pages and allow users the option of downloading and browsing at their leisure using their Internet Web browsing tool.

3. Establish benefits early

What motivates people to buy a product or service? People are first and foremost drawn to the benefits that your product or service will bring to them. In most cases, products and services are sold on only one or two specific benefits or a brand name, and all the other benefits listed are not considered very important. While customers are fresh at your site, you must clearly identify the key benefits of your product or service. These benefits should be referred to at the beginning of the visit and reinforced whenever possible throughout the site visit. You may have many different personality types visiting your site, including those who are impulsive, opinionated, skeptical, methodical, procrastinating, or grouchy. You will need to cater to these various types of people during your electronic sales presentation.

Business tip:
On-line catalogues — Do it yourself!

Creating a multimedia catalogue is no longer the domain of the specialist. Today, there are inexpensive computer programs that allow anyone with a PC to prepare professional-looking electronic catalogues.

Web-based catalogues can be prepared using the Internet Creator, by Forman Interactive. This program sells for approximately $149 and runs under Windows on any 386 PC. This tool lets you easily create great-looking on-line catalogues. Forman Interactive also offers Web space for $57 a month to allow users of the software to get on-line quickly and economically.

Forman Interactive
201 Water Street
Brooklyn, NY 11201
Tel: (718) 522-2260
http://www.forman.com/
Software: Internet Creator

Downloadable catalogues may be readily prepared using the Prostar Minicat system. This program sells for approximately $200 and runs under Windows on any 386 PC. Prostar Minicat allows you to integrate up to 100 images and 800 pages of text into a menu-based catalogue browsing system. Prostar also provides a service to help distribute catalogues that were created using the Minicat program.

Prostar Interactive Media Works
13880 Mayfield Place
Richmond, B.C. V6V 2E4
mailto:sales@prostar-int.com
http://prostar-int.com
Software: Minicat

Once you have caught your customers' attention with the benefits, they will likely want to probe further into different features, variations in product models that you support, and options on the individual models themselves. Your product catalogue and menu system must effectively summarize the product's or service's features, and more detailed information should be available either through your site or by contacting the company through e-mail or by telephone.

Last, customers want to know about product warranties, service options, and installation or repair costs. Provide customers with enough information so that they won't consider such information an issue as they decide whether to purchase your product or service.

If you plan to support an electronic catalogue, you should examine BBSs as well as check out software on the market that will make your job a lot easier.

4. Anticipate your customers' questions

The different people visiting your site will have a variety of questions that will need to be answered by your electronic sales pitch. How should you answer them and deal with potential sales objections?

You will need to plan ahead and provide enough information on your electronic site so that various customers will be able to browse through your menus to review your products' features and feature descriptions. You could also use the FAQ (frequently asked questions) approach, which models the common Internet FAQs that are well known in the Internet community. Using the FAQ approach, you would provide a list of questions and answers that might cover 90% of the questions arising from customers' visits. Have your service or sales personnel generate this company FAQ list, since they are most familiar with questions normally asked by customers.

Another way to anticipate your customers' questions is to provide an e-mail or question submission form that allows the customer to ask questions which your sales or service teams can respond to. If you do this, be sure that you can turn around responses quickly and that you can answer responses effectively. These questions can be used to feedback into the sales and service process to build new product features, develop more effective sales presentations, or further enhance your FAQ list.

Business tip:
What e-mail addresses to make public

In much the same way as businesses publish telephone numbers for specific departments to guide customers to appropriate staff, many on-line businesses publish general contact e-mail addresses, such as *product-support@widgets. com, helpdesk@widgets.com, sales@widgets.com, service@ widgets.com, info@widgets.com*, and *suggestions@widgets.com*, which are read and managed by the appropriate staff. In general, it is not a good idea to publish e-mail addresses of employees as the customers' point of contact, since employees may come and go.

Key to success

Keep control of e-mail customer interactions

E-mail is a direct conduit through which customers may send a message to company employees who otherwise are not involved in direct customer contact. It is important to decide how employees will interact with customers using e-mail and who should be authorized to do so.

5. Provide a simple, secure ordering and billing mechanism

One of the major concerns of the Internet community is the security of credit transactions over the network. Making your billing system flexible and easy to use will help grease the wheels to a sale. Details on how to provide a secure and flexible ordering system are found below.

6. Provide an active customer feedback mechanism

E-mail, or Web tools incorporating e-mail, can provide you with an excellent customer feedback mechanism. Internet users are generally willing to provide feedback on both your site and your products. A curious characteristic of e-mail and electronic communication media is that users tend to provide both frank and useful input if you ask them for it. Providing open feedback forms, more structured survey forms, or a simple telephone number will allow your site to grow and mature to become a more powerful marketing tool for your company. It will also provide an outlet for your potential customers to express themselves and, at the same time, provide you with another candidate for your mailing lists.

7. Allow for human contact

As business and on-line users run faster into the electronic future, the need for human contact will grow and possibly become a feature of your business. The ability to support interpersonal contacts will project the image that even though you are a leading edge company, you still care about the individual.

There are various ways to achieve this, including using e-mail or a toll-free telephone line so that your customers can talk directly to your customer service or sales representative, who can then answer any lingering questions.

d. Closing and processing a sale

Once the customer has decided to purchase your product, you need to make it easy for the transaction to occur. There are two main steps to this process that you should incorporate into your business operation. You should allow for secure transactions (both manual and electronic), and you should allow for multiple product orders to be made in a single session.

1. Allow for secure transactions

Your Internet customers are acutely aware of the security problems related to on-line transactions. As a business operator, you should be aware that you are liable for any charges incurred because of fraudulent use of credit cards. Let's examine the four main methods of billing that are available to provide a flexible but secure environment.

(a) **Indirect ordering/payment:** The customer uses traditional methods such as a fax order form or a toll-free telephone number to place an order. This method is the same as that used for mail order today, and provides a good level of security for both the merchant and customer.

(b) **Direct ordering/indirect payment:** The customer fills out an electronic order form but does not include the credit card number or expiry date information. You must telephone the customer to obtain the credit card information and verify the order. This method is fairly secure and provides a good fit to the current order management processes.

(c) **Direct ordering/direct account payment:** The customer orders products on-line from a company where the customer already has pre-approved credit. The customer has a membership ID number so that the orders can be processed and shipped. Orders may be verified by manually telephoning the customer. This technique is good for wholesale to retail relationships and is convenient for the customer, but requires management of individual customer accounts. There are some security issues surrounding the use of stolen ID numbers.

(d) **Direct ordering/direct payment:** This is the most advanced technique and it allows the transfer of credit information over the network. Encryption technology is used for the credit information security, and authentification technology for proof of electronic signatures of the customers. New electronic Internet mercantile protocols are being developed, but are still experimental at this stage and will require a more sophisticated billing and customer order management system.

A discussion of electronic cash, or e-cash, can be found in chapter 7. Also see "Understanding security issues" in chapter 5.

2. Allow for multiple product orders to be made in a single session

Just like in any store operation, you want the customer to purchase as many items as possible. To accommodate this, you need to set up your ordering system to accept multiple items at a single purchase session, so that your customer need use only a single key stroke. The Web, Telnet, Gopher, and e-mail are four tools that perform this function; we recommend the Web.

e. Handling after-sales service

"A bird in the hand is worth two in the bush" is an old adage that refers to making the best of what you have now, rather than focusing on what you don't have. This is very much the case when dealing with your current Internet customer base. These customers are valuable and you don't want them to vanish into cyberspace because you haven't continued to treat them like valued customers after their initial purchase of your product or service. How should you go about providing excellent after-sales service?

The first question you need to answer is, "Why are my Internet customers contacting me?" There may be a number of reasons, including the following:

On-line transactions and security *

- Eighty-two percent of Internet customers view security of financial information as a major issue.

- The majority of users consider it foolish to provide credit information on-line.

- Most customers cite transaction security as the main reason they don't buy on-line.

- Most customers consider toll-free phone/fax or secure transmission more desirable than e-mail.

- Most users would like a third party involved when dealing with Web vendors.

- Most users would prefer credit card companies and banks as their first choice of a third party; their last choice is an unknown mall operator.

GTRC 1995 survey

(a) They are experiencing some particular problem with your product.

(b) They didn't read the manual and they want to save their time and use yours.

(c) They want to find out more about your product's capabilities.

(d) They are considering ordering more products and have questions.

All of these are valid reasons for calling, though your service representative may get tired of answering the same old questions. Even though on-line business is a faceless transaction, customers still need to be treated as though they are standing right in front of you.

Most queries will arrive at your service center via e-mail, and your service representatives will need to respond in a professional and friendly manner. One of the techniques that you will need to instill in your service people is the correct use of e-mail for responding in nonthreatening and nonconfrontational ways. This is not always easy in an impersonal electronic environment.

Here are some tips for creating a professional image:

(a) Never respond to angry e-mails with anger or ego.

(b) Always explain the information or situation in a friendly manner.

(c) Thank your customers whenever possible for their patronage.

(d) Use the telephone instead of e-mail if the situation is complicated.

(e) Try to go the extra distance to make service a selling feature of your business.

> ### Business tip:
> ### E-mail usage
>
> The immediacy of e-mail is both a blessing and a curse. E-mail can be read and responded to in a short period. This inherently makes impulsive and emotional responses a real danger. With traditional paper-based business correspondence, the time delay in the process allows for an ill-considered response to be reworked. With e-mail, impulsiveness can be indulged.
>
> A good rule to follow with e-mail is to never hit the "send" key if you have just written a message that may be tainted by emotion of the moment — leave the message on the computer until the next day, and review it again before sending it on its way.
>
> E-mail lends itself to conversational and sometimes impersonal interactions. In face-to-face discussions or telephone conversations, potential misinterpretations can be cleared up immediately. With e-mail, a casual tone with someone other than a friend can lead to misunderstandings or incorrect impressions about you and your business because there is no context or avenue for clarification. E-mail correspondence must be approached as carefully as any other business interaction.
>
> Carefully consider the image you want to express externally, and the impact on your potential customers — and be consistent.

When setting up a sales or after-sales support service on the Internet, be sure to manage customer expectations appropriately. In particular, if you provide an e-mail address to which customer complaints or requests for help may be directed, be absolutely sure that you either respond to the e-mail in a timely manner (within a week, for example), or publicize when (or if) customers using the service can expect a response to a query.

As a case in point, we purchased some PC software which touted an e-mail address to which questions related to the product could be directed. We ran into some problems when trying to use the software as described in the manual. We directed several queries over a three-week period to the published e-mail address, but never received any response. The support e-mail address was a black hole from which no help and only frustration emerged. Needless to say, customer satisfaction was very low.

The approaches to creating, advertising, marketing, and operating your Internet presence on a daily business should aim to keep your customers coming back to your site.

9.

Selecting and building your Internet service platform

By now, you probably have a few ideas about how you would like to use the Internet. The next question is likely "What next?"

What's next is to decide what you need to do in order to get your business on the Internet. There are several items that you will need to make decisions on, including:

(a) whether to work with a consultant,

(b) what Internet platform to use,

(c) what your Internet access requirements are,

(d) which Internet service provider you should use, and

(e) what your ongoing maintenance plans are.

a. Should I work with a consultant?

Working with consultants to set up and maintain your Internet presence is an expedient way to get your business on the Internet. Working with a consultant can have a number of advantages. For instance, an article in the April 3, 1995, issue of *Information Week* reported on both Visa's and General Electric's decisions to contract out their Web presences. A Visa spokesperson indicated that out-sourcing was more cost effective than taking the job on internally. The General Electric spokesperson, on the other hand, felt that the value of working with consultants came from the expertise and different perspectives brought to the table.

Be sure to ask any consultant you are considering hiring for references first. If you are hiring consultants to author your business's Web or Gopher sites, always ask to see examples of work that they have done for others in the past.

If you do not wish to work with a consultant, you might consider choosing a specific vendor, working with its sales personnel to develop a system configuration that matches its needs, or you could work with your ISP to develop and maintain your Internet presence.

b. Should I lease or own my Internet platform?

If your business is based on e-mail or is for browsing Internet resources, you will need a computer, a modem, and a data communications program (see chapter 2). You will also need to determine your Internet access requirements and to choose an appropriate ISP (described later in this chapter).

If you want to provide a 24-hour Internet presence (e.g., a Web site, Telnet-based BBS, Gopher site, or FTP archive), you will need a computer system that is permanently connected to the Internet. You have two options: rent the required Internet resources from a third party, or purchase, install, and maintain your own system.

If you decide to lease your Internet services, there are many companies available to work with you. Leasing may be more economical than owning and is a good way to test the waters.

If you decide to own your own platform, you will need to select and configure your chosen hardware and software combination. Setting up and owning your own Internet presence requires a significant commitment in terms of fixed and recurring costs.

1. Leasing

For many businesses, renting Internet resources from another company may be the best way to get on-line quickly. (However, you will still need an ISP in order to access the Internet and the mall where you choose to rent space.) There are various types of Internet presence that can be rented. Options range from electronic malls to virtual sites which look and act as if you were operating from equipment installed at your business premises.

(a) Electronic mall

If you want to set up shop on an electronic mall, you should look for the following information from the vendor:

- How many customers visit the mall and how are these figures verified? Can the vendor provide you with a computer printout characterizing recent activity at the mall site, as well as your business's storefront in the mall?

- What is done to publicize the electronic mall location? What type of print advertising is done? What sort of Internet-based advertising is done (e.g., does it have hotlinks in place with popular Internet sites)? In which Internet directory services or business lists is the electronic mall listed?

- How does the vendor know that the mall has enough bandwidth to the Internet? Can the vendor provide you with usage statistics on its communications link to the Internet? Many malls share their Internet connections with other users and applications. If the connection is regularly hitting close to 100% utilization, it is not big enough and you can count on customers staying away due to electronic traffic jams.

- How long have existing storefronts been in place? A high turnover in mall residents is a sure sign that the mall is not generating profits for the tenants.

- How are sales transacted with customers? Does the mall provide a secure method for customers to send credit card and mailing information? A secure payment method may make the mall more attractive to on-line shoppers by making it easier to transact business all at once, rather than having to spend additional time with faxes or on the telephone.

- What do the existing mall tenants have to say? Are they happy with their investment? Are they seeing increased sales due to their on-line presence? Are they satisfied with the support and service from the mall owners?

- What are other mall tenants selling? Are their services likely to draw customers who would be attracted to your storefront as well, or are you likely to be competing head to head with the other storefronts? Does the mall have a policy in place so that it doesn't accept other stores that will compete with you?

- Do the stores cater toward local, regional, national, or global sales? Does the mall support multiple languages? A multilingual mall may increase your potential market.

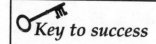

Key to success

Finding electronic malls
The best way to find an appropriate electronic mall is to either work with a consultant, or go on-line yourself. If you choose the latter route, the best place to start looking is at The Shopper — *http://www.hummsoft.com/ hummsoft/shopper.html* .

This Internet site provides descriptions and reviews for over 370 electronic malls.

If you plan to sell to customers in France and Mexico, for example, an English-only mall is unlikely to attract a large number of potential customers.

- What are the costs? Are there any setup fees or monthly fees? Does your store have to pay a percentage of sales to the mall?

The cost of leasing space on an electronic mall can range from a few hundred to several thousand dollars a month. The rates charged usually depend on the number of stores in the mall and the number of customers visiting the site. Shop around and be sure to pick a mall that matches your market requirements.

Business tip:
Counting visitors to
World Wide Web-based malls

If your business's electronic mall rent is based on the number of customers that visit, you should be aware that methods used for measuring the number of real visitors to Web-based malls are in their infancy. There has been much contention in the Internet community about various traffic claims. Before signing up with an electronic mall, ensure that the mall operator clearly explains how real mall customers are being estimated and measured.

For example, electronic malls will typically advertise the number of *hits* that they receive. In Web documents, one page of hypertext may contain text and any number of graphic images. If a page contains some text and three images, when someone looks at that page, four hits will be generated: one for the text content of the page and one for each image. The number of hits is not necessarily equivalent to the number of customers.

(b) Virtual site

Virtual sites offer the flexibility for your business to set up an Internet presence indistinguishable from anything that you could set up on your own computer system. Companies that offer virtual site services for business are called Internet presence providers and can provide any type of Internet service required, including FTP sites, e-mailing lists, Gopher sites, and e-mail information servers. Internet presence providers may offer all, or any combination, of the following:

- Domain name registration for your company

- Internet authoring

- Marketing/publicity of your Internet business

- Dedicated computer hardware

- On-going maintenance

If you want to set up a Web site using the services of an Internet presence provider, there are four typical steps you would go through.

(a) Decide on the Internet domain name for your company.

(b) Decide on content and functionality of the Web site.

(c) Decide on whether to pay for dedicated equipment to be installed and maintained at the Internet presence provider's premises, or whether to simply share space on one of its existing computer systems.

(d) Agree on a maintenance contract that may include reports on how many people visited your business site and content updates.

You can find Internet presence providers by contacting your ISP, working with a consultant, or performing an on-line search using one of the directories listed in chapter 4, or the Yahoo IPP directory.

2. Owning

A typical Internet business site physically consists of a computer system (which runs programs supporting your Internet business presence and is usually not used for any other purpose) and communications equipment (to connect the computer to the Internet).

(a) Computer system

Your choice of computer system and software is wide open, and will be based on the number of customers and type of services you expect to support. The most popular computer systems used for Internet business sites are IBM compatible PC systems and Unix workstations (e.g., Sun Microsystems and clones). PC systems generally tend to be less expensive than Unix workstations in terms of hardware, software, and maintenance costs.

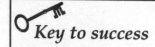

Key to success

Set up your Internet presence — virtually anywhere!

When it comes to setting up your Internet presence, you do not need to purchase your virtual site from a local provider. On the Internet, the physical location of your presence doesn't matter. This gives you the flexibility to find the best deal, regardless of where your business is located.

Internet presence providers

Yahoo Directory
http://www.yahoo.com/Business_ and_Economy/Companies/Internet_ Presence_Providers

If your business already has the necessary technical expertise, you can easily put together your own hardware and software package. If not, you should purchase a preconfigured system such as described later in this chapter. Alternatively, you might contract selection and installation to an appropriate computer consultant.

Business tip:
Mature software technology

BBSs are already well established and have a large base of users. Bulletin board software technology is generally robust, having been optimized over a number of years to cater to on-line, text-based services such as electronic catalogues. Most software can support several simultaneous customer sessions using inexpensive IBM AT-type (an old IBM PC model) PCs. The setup and maintenance of such systems is generally more straightforward than the Unix-based systems traditionally used for Internet services. BBSs tend to be oriented toward dial-up modem users, and in the last few years, all the major bulletin board software manufacturers have introduced, or stated their intention to support, upgrades that allow their software to be readily integrated with the Internet.

If you are planning to offer an electronic catalogue using the Telnet tool, we recommend that you seriously evaluate using a traditional BBS as the basis for your on-line presence. Two companies offering bulletin board software that is well suited for on-line electronic catalogues are —

Clark Development Company, Inc.
3950 South 700 East, Suite 303
Murray, UT 84107-2173   Tel: (801) 261-1686
mailto:sales@saltair.com
http://www.pcboard.com
Software package: PCBoard

Galacticomm Inc.
4104 S.W. 47th Avenue, Suite 101
Fort Lauderdale, FL 33314   Tel: (800) 328-1128
mailto:sales@gcomm.com
http://www.gcomm.com/
Software package: Galacticomm

Business tip:
Shoestring Unix-based Internet business platform

If you want to set up a shoestring operation and are an experienced computer user, consider using a PC running the Linux operating system. The hardware requirements are modest, requiring only a 386/33 Mhz PC configured with 8 Mb of RAM, 80 Mb hard drive, a CD-ROM drive, and a 28.8 Kbps modem. Using this platform, you can offer FTP, WAIS, Gopher, Telnet, and Web services.

The book *Building a Unix Internet Server* by George Eckel (Indianapolis: New Riders Publishing, 1995) provides you with both the software (on a CD-ROM) and the detailed instructions necessary to get your system up and running. However, be warned that this approach is not for the meek of heart!

If you don't have any computer experts on staff and you want to get an Internet business site up and running as fast as possible, your best bet is to purchase one of the many available preconfigured Internet business site packages. Purchasing an out-of-the-box system is an effective way to establish an Internet presence quickly.

Preconfigured systems include all the computer hardware and software necessary to set up shop on the Internet. Some setups will even be preconfigured before being shipped to your business location. When considering all-inclusive Internet site packages, you have the option of choosing from setups that are based on professional-quality Unix workstations to systems based on comparatively inexpensive PCs. Preconfigured systems start at $4,000 for a low-end system using PC technology, jumping to $10,000 and higher for high-end Unix workstation-based solutions. In general, the high-end systems offer greater capacity: a greater number of simultaneous customers may be supported.

(b) Communications equipment

For dial-up connections, all that is required is a modem. However, if you plan to build an Internet platform which is permanently connected to the Internet, you will need a dedicated dial-up or leased-line connection.

Internet business packages vendors

Sun Microsystems
(Netra Internet server)
http://www.sun.com/

Bitwise Internet Technologies
(Bitserver)
http://www.bitwise.net/
mailto:sales@bitwise.net

Silicon Graphics Inc
(WebFORCE)
http://www.sgi.com/

Integrix
http://www.integrix.com
mailto:sales@integrix.com

> **Minimum access speed**
> For E-mail, Telnet, Gopher, WAIS, FTP, the Web (text-only)
> - 2,400 bps (shell account)
>
> For Web usage (multimedia)
> - 14,400 bps (SLIP/PPP account)

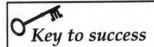

Key to success

Reducing your Internet access costs

For each unique e-mail address that a business supports, a SLIP, PPP, or shell account is usually required. If your business has more than one person who uses e-mail, you should shop around for an ISP that offers the option of having more than one e-mail address associated with the login account. This economical service is not available from all OSPs or ISPs.

When it comes to high-speed leased lines of 56 Kbps and higher, the equipment you will need will often be recommended, and possibly even supplied, by your ISP. You may need to special order this equipment from a telephone or telecommunications equipment company. Have your ISP install and test this equipment at your business site and show you how to check that the equipment is working correctly.

Chapter 2 has additional details on Internet access and the various communications equipment, such as dedicated dial-up modems and leased-line connections, available to you.

c. Determining Internet access requirements

The next step is to determine the type of access that your business application needs. If you are planning to use the Internet for e-mail-based business applications, or as a resource that is available as you need it, then a shared dial-up may be your best option. In general, a 28.8 Kbps access speed is preferable for dial-up access.

A shared dial-up connection may be purchased for $20 per month or less. If you do not want the possibility of having to wait to connect to the Internet, you will want to investigate a dedicated dial-up connection.

If you plan to offer a 24-hour service for your customers using anything except e-mail, you will need a dedicated or leased connection to the Internet from whatever computer system is providing the service. For dedicated Internet connections, the access speed required is based on a number of factors, primarily the number of simultaneous customers you expect to support and the Internet tools used to implement the service. You will need to contact your ISP to determine the best access speed for your specific needs.

In general, however, you will want to ensure that your computer system and software are matched to the bandwidth of the connection. This information is usually available from the commercial software vendor. It won't be cost efficient to buy a T1 leased line if your computer system and software are able to use only 50% of the bandwidth of the T1.

d. Selecting an Internet service provider (ISP)

There are a wide range of ISPs to choose from, with the number of providers having increased significantly in the last two years. This rapid growth has brought with it a wide range of fee structures and service quality. We recommend that you spend the time to make a careful selection of your ISP. By taking some extra time initially, you may avoid having to waste time relocating to another service provider because of poor or mismatched service expectations. When selecting an ISP, you should evaluate the following:

(a) Scope of service

(b) Cost structure

(c) Acceptable-use policy

(d) User support

(e) Software

(f) User training

(g) Internet access

(h) Reliability

(i) Service portfolio

(j) Trial runs

(k) Bonded employees

The first step when considering an ISP is to ask for a copy of its corporate background and service agreement. The next step is to review this information against each consideration above.

1. Scope of service

What is the market scope of the service provider? Is the Internet service offered on an international, national, regional, or local basis? It is argued by some that the best service is likely to come from small local service providers, since they need to differentiate themselves from larger service providers that have a seemingly infinite advertising budget. However, the reality is that you can get good Internet service from a service provider of any market scope.

There are valid reasons for choosing a regional, national, or international service provider, particularly if you are planning to use the Internet extensively between business sites. If you chose a regional, national, or international service, you can have

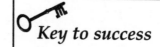

Key to success

Make the most of your Internet connection

If you have a dedicated Internet connection to your business site, you may want to consider reselling your Internet service. If your business is co-located with other businesses that want Internet access, you may be able to recoup some of the set up and monthly charges. In effect, you will become a service provider yourself!

all your business sites using the same ISP. Depending on the number of business sites you plan to hook up to the Internet, it may be possible to negotiate a better deal on access charges by securing a volume discount. Having all your business sites with the same provider can also simplify billings. However, the biggest benefit will be when your business runs into problems with the Internet connection between your sites. If all your business locations use the same service provider, your life will be easier, since the number of suppliers that you need to coordinate with in order to resolve a problem is reduced.

Another consideration is the nature of the customer base that the ISP caters to. If it caters primarily to business customers, it would be reasonable to expect that you will receive a high quality of service since the provider will be better acquainted with the needs and expectations of Internet business users.

2. Cost structure

There are a wide variety of pricing and access options available, and not all are necessarily available from every provider. There is no standard or government regulation when it comes to Internet access charging. To protect yourself from any unpleasant surprises, you need to understand exactly how the ISP charges for services. In particular, scrutinize any services that have usage-based charges. CompuServe, for example, charges a monthly flat rate and a connect charge billed by the minute. Only basic services are covered under the flat-rate charge.

From a pure cost perspective, if you are serious about doing business on the Internet, your best bet is to avoid the large OSPs and look at those businesses specializing in offering Internet access. For dial-up business applications, the best approach is to purchase service from a provider that offers flat-rate charges (i.e., so much a month for so many hours of connect time per month, period).

To ensure that you have a comprehensive view of potential charges, you should have answers to all of the following questions:

(a) Is there a setup fee and if so, how much? Is the charge per user account or per business?

(b) What is the monthly access fee? Is there a discount available if the access fees are paid for in advance (e.g., a yearly subscription fee)?

(c) How many hours of connect time are included in the monthly fee? What is the incremental hourly rate for connect time above the base amount? How are connect times calculated and how will any discrepancies in connect time between you and the ISP be resolved?

(d) Are there any usage-based fees (e.g., e-mail messages, disk space, Web-page use)? How are usage-based fees calculated and, again, how will any discrepancies between you and the ISP be resolved?

(e) What billing mechanism is used? Does the ISP make charges to your credit card on a monthly basis? How detailed is the bill? Will it be easy for you to rationalize the bill with your personal usage records?

(f) Does the ISP offer toll-free access outside your local area? Is there an additional access premium and if so, what is it?

3. Acceptable-use policy

Many ISPs have their own version of an acceptable-use policy, intended to protect the service provider from legal actions resulting from activities of its customers. In some cases, the policy is used as a subtle way to place restrictions on the use of Internet access by the customer.

Before you sign a service agreement with your ISP, carefully review any acceptable-use policy that the service provider may have. In particular, look for any fine print that may constrain your business use of the Internet access. Some service providers offer free Web pages for all users, but have fine print limiting the number of monthly accesses allowed, charging for any additional accesses. Some service providers limit the type of business you can do with your account, to prevent you from competing directly with them. For example, you may be prohibited from reselling your Internet access to others.

Other service providers may restrict your use of Web scripts called *CGIs* (see chapter 3), which provide a great deal of flexibility to the business user, particularly when used with the forms capability of the Web. This type of restriction can really limit your creativity. Other providers may allow the use of Web scripts, but will charge extra fees for each script or for subsequent changes to existing scripts.

4. User support

If you are new to computers, modems, and data communications programs, you and your employees are going to have questions such as, "I can't seem to connect to the Internet, what's wrong?" and "How do I set up my Internet tool software?" You can plan to hire a consultant or live with the reduced productivity as you and your staff dig through reference books, or you can ensure that you have a user-friendly ISP on your side.

When you are evaluating ISPs, find out what kind of help you and your staff can expect. Here are some good questions to ask:

- What type of user support is provided (e.g., telephone helpline, e-mail helpline)? What are the hours of operation for the telephone helpline? What is the typical response time for queries sent to the e-mail helpline?

- What type of questions or problems is the ISP willing to support, and what software tools and computer types (PC or Macintosh) are supported?

- Is any documentation available to users? Are on-line "how-to's" or tutorial information provided? (A good ISP will provide you with a step-by-step written guide on how to set up your software, as well as answers to common problems that you are likely to encounter.)

- Does the ISP offer on-site support as an option? What does it offer and how much does it cost?

It may be a good investment to have the ISP come on site to your business to install and test your Internet hardware and access software. With a little negotiation, you may find that some ISPs, particularly the regional or local providers, are willing to offer this service in return for your company's patronage.

5. Software

Many ISPs offer free software as part of their package. This can help reduce the costs of getting your Internet business off the ground. Some questions to consider include:

- Is any access software provided to new users? What computer type is the software provided for? Are there any additional charges for the software provided? If the software is shareware, what are the terms for use and purchasing?

- Does the ISP provide setup profile information for other popular Internet access software? Does it offer any discounts on commercial software packages?

6. User training

Regardless of the size of your business, training on how to use the Internet tools software may help to rapidly advance productivity. You will find that some local ISPs offer free training sessions as part of their service package, to differentiate themselves from the larger national ISPs.

7. Internet access

The speed of the link that connects your service provider's system to the Internet is an important consideration, particularly if you are dealing with a local or regional service provider. Your ISP will use a leased-line connection to another, larger, ISP that provides service between cities or internationally. The speed that connects your ISP with the other ISP is not necessarily the same as that connecting you to your ISP. Generally, business-oriented ISPs have a high bandwidth connection (full T1, multiple T1s, or T3) to the Internet.

If you are only looking for e-mail service, then a 56 Kbps link to the Internet will generally be sufficient. However, if you are expecting to make use of other Internet services, such as the Web, then a T1 or higher connection is desirable.

A point of caution is worth noting here: some ISPs advertise a T1 access to the Internet when, in reality, all they have is a *fractional T1* link. A full T1 access is the equivalent of 1.544 Mbps. A fractional T1 link allocates only a portion of the T1 link to the ISP, and can range in speed from 56 Kbps to 1.544 Mbps. The best way to be sure is to ask the service provider how much bandwidth of the T1 is actually being used to carry Internet data traffic.

If you want to purchase a dial-up account from the ISP, you need to ask about their ratio of dial-up lines to users. A reasonable ratio is generally considered to be one dial-up line for every ten dial-up users registered with the service. Also find out at what periods of the day all dial-up lines are in use for shared dial-up access lines. If the ISP regularly has all dial-up lines in use during the periods of the day that you expect to need access, perhaps this service provider isn't the best choice.

If you or your staff travel extensively, another consideration will be whether the ISP offers a toll-free access number.

8. Reliability

Is the service being run as a full-time commercial venture or as a part-time activity out of someone's residence? Is the ISP an informal business or an established commercial enterprise? A part-time activity is unlikely to provide the same degree of reliability as a commercial activity with dedicated staff.

Does the ISP have a backup plan in the event of equipment failure? Ideally, you should sign up with a service provider that has duplicate computer hardware for providing SLIP/PPP, shell accounts, or for offering any virtual site services. Does it maintain regular backup copies of any files that reside on its computer system? If your service provider doesn't have a file backup strategy, then you chance losing your files if there is a technical mistake or equipment failure.

Does the ISP have a security policy? Does it perform regular audits of its system to check for holes, using automated tools (such as SATAN) that test the security of Internet computers? If the service provider doesn't take security seriously, its system and any of your files residing on its system are at risk of being compromised (e.g., modified, stolen, or deleted).

Finally, how many users currently subscribe to this service? A service provider with few users may not be around for too long, or conversely, you may have to endure growing pains as the provider expands and adds new equipment and staff.

9. Service portfolio

If you have plans to increase your Internet business, you should look for an ISP with which you can grow. What incremental services can the ISP offer your business? For example, does it offer domain name registration, leased-line services, Web authoring, virtual servers, or custom newsgroup setup and management?

10. Trial runs

Before you commit yourself to a particular ISP, ask for a free trial run of the service. Does the service provider offer any on-site demonstrations? Does it offer trial accounts that you can use for a few weeks? If so, take advantage of its offer and evaluate on-line quality firsthand.

A good place to get feedback from existing customers of the service provider is to browse the service provider-specific newsgroups that are often in place. Dissatisfied customers of the service provider often post their experiences and opinions of the quality of the service. Determine whether any complaints are in fact chronic problems with the service provider, or simply a problem with the way a user is using the service.

11. Bonded employees

Your ISP will implicitly have the ability to access any electronic data passing into and out of your business. To help reduce the risk of being compromised, it is a good idea to use a service provider that uses only bonded employees.

e. Where to find Internet service providers

Armed with an understanding of what you should be looking for, the next step is to find a service provider that matches your needs. A good place to start is your local telephone Yellow Pages under "data communication." As well, if you have on-line access to the Internet already, or know someone who does, you can retrieve comprehensive lists of providers from Internet resources like Yahoo and The List.

ISP directories

Yahoo Directory
http://www.yahoo.com/Business/ Corporations/Internet_Access_ Providers/

The List
http://thelist.com

f. Ongoing maintenance

Once your Internet business presence is on-line, you may be faced with two major sources of ongoing maintenance costs: computer system maintenance and information maintenance.

If you have set up your own Internet business site, you will need to maintain the computer hardware and software. The computer hardware is usually managed on a failure basis, and repair work contracted out to local repair shops. This cost is difficult to predict in advance, although it may be mitigated by purchasing extended warranties and site-service plans. Downtime as a consequence of a failure can be minimized by having a service agreement in place with a local repair company. The best approach, though it may be more costly, is to have a repair service that offers on-site repair within 24 hours.

Aside from the computer hardware itself, the software running on the computer needs regular monitoring and maintenance. The types of maintenance activities necessary vary between the operating systems and application software used. Staff or contracted support are necessary to reconfigure software for any new hardware, monitor the system to ensure that all the software is operating as expected, ensure that the computer system recovers from power failures or reboots, schedule and perform file backup and restoration, and clean out computer-specific information logs. These tasks are specific to the computer and its general operation. For single-computer sites, this support activity may be assigned as a part-time task for an existing employee. For multicomputer sites, this support easily requires one or more full-time, skilled employees to run and maintain.

Regardless of whether you set up your own computer site on the Internet or lease a space or a virtual site from a third party, you will be faced with support costs for your on-line presence. As with any business, change is an inevitable part of life. The information content or services will need ongoing updating and revision to reflect product or price changes. For leased or virtual sites, content maintenance may be addressed to a certain degree in the service agreement with your Internet presence provider. If it is not covered in the service agreement, it will likely appear as a surprise charge the first time you approach your service provider and request an update. We recommend that content revision and update services be captured in your contract.

10.

Vision of the future

The global computer, telecommunications, and cable television businesses are currently in the midst of massive changes caused primarily by the deregulation of telecommunications networks around the world. The United States was the first to see the turmoil in 1984, as AT&T broke into seven separate "Baby Bell" local telephone companies, Bell Communications Research (Bellcore), and its huge long distance operation, AT&T Communications. MCI and Sprint long distance carriers joined the fray and have gradually established the highly competitive long distance market environment that we are now seeing today. U.S. deregulation started similar government reactions in Canada, the United Kingdom, continental Europe, and Central and South America, and has now spread worldwide, leading to restructuring of telecommunications into more competitive markets.

As deregulation was occurring, the telecommunications giants recognized the lucrative cable television market as an opportunity for competition. Both telecommunications and cable television companies are now proposing to provide multimedia interactive services to the home and business, with capabilities far outstripping what is currently offered.

Computer vendors have eyed this as an opportunity for possible deployment of more computing devices into homes and businesses, in a direction they hope will lead to greater profitability. The ubiquitous home and business computers have been at the center of all this excitement, with higher processing speeds, larger disk sizes, greater memory, more powerful computer operating systems (DOS, Windows, Windows NT, and UNIX), and better computer interfaces to access networks like Internet, commercial on-line services, and BBSs.

What's driving this turmoil? The vision of an information-based society and the electronic economy. Visionaries see a society that will operate with an increased amount of voice, data, and video communications to conduct global businesses. Software applications like desk-to-desk video conferencing, multiparty video conferencing, distance learning, electronic medical imaging, interactive entertainment, and electronic education are at the center of the new environment. To allow such applications to work, high performance networks must form an information superhighway. This highway will be the main artery over which all the video, data, and voice traffic will be carried.

It is no wonder that the Internet has garnered high interest from the various telecommunications, computer, and cable television companies, and now entertainment and media companies. The Internet, while currently very small in comparison to these other markets, contains all the technological elements of a new information-based economy. The past success of the Internet has been based on the key ideas of transparent and universal access for users to a network comprised of interconnected networks. The strength of the Internet has been its ability to adapt to the growing range of user needs and applications for which it is being used. These farsighted principles have allowed the Internet's unparalleled growth and the accommodation of millions of new users desiring access.

One of the current shortcomings of the Internet, however, is that the communications links to access the network from your home are limited to 28.8 Kbps modems on a standard telephone line. This limits the speed at which graphics and text information can be downloaded to your computer terminal and ultimately what you can do with the information offered by content providers operating on the network. Businesses do not have this limitation if they are already using local area network (LAN) or wide area network (WAN) technology. How will issues like higher speed access be solved? How will the different business players affect the evolution of the Internet and your business as part of this global phenomenon?

In the following sections, we provide a view of where we believe the Internet is going with the creation of the information superhighway and, in particular, how the Internet fits in.

a. Internet growth

The keyword of the future is GROWTH! Internet growth is expected to increase even more than it has in the past couple of years with the massive new numbers of novice Internet users joining the global electronic community. Estimates are that by the year 2000, there will be 100 to 150 million users, up from the current 30 million plus users. As the network grows, increasing portions of your business will have to cater to the demands of the on-line consumer.

b. Internet tools evolution

The creation of more sophisticated network browsers exceeding the capabilities of Netscape and Mosaic will generate increasingly more sophisticated applications on the Web, using more powerful communications protocols. Current text-based tools like Gopher, WAIS, and Veronica will gradually fade away as consumers get used to the high graphical content of the Web tools. Many of these browsers will eventually become part of the software provided with computer purchases, much the same way as Windows, DOS, and some applications programs are provided with PCs today. As these graphical tools evolve, you will need to keep pace to ensure that your Internet presence is kept looking modern.

c. Types of computers accessing the Internet

Originally, UNIX-based computers were the mainstay of the Internet. Now PCs and Macintoshes are becoming the dominant ones. This trend puts increasing pressure on computer vendors offering UNIX platforms to keep in lockstep with PC developments.

d. Establishment of an effective Internet business directory

The problem of the lack of an effective directory service will be solved as small and big companies start conducting increasing amounts of business over the Internet. Chaos precedes organization, as was the case in the taming of the wild west, and this is one area where directory services technology in the telecommunications world will help out Internet-based businesses very effectively.

e. Security of business transactions

Visa, MasterCard, and all major banking institutions are currently working on developing secure Internet mercantile protocols which will allow credit card numbers, expiry dates, and personal identification numbers (PINs) to be safely transmitted over the Internet. In the next few years, this issue will start to be actively addressed in the large on-line catalogue shopping market. Once such protocols are developed, further opportunities for the large on-line catalogue operators will be created.

f. Internet economics: Introduction of a user-pay model

Currently, access to the Internet is charged according to the amount of time connected to the network and sometimes by speed of the connection. No attempt has been made to charge explicitly for the amount of network resources consumed. The ISPs today are typically providing modem access ranging in speed from 9.6 Kbps to 28.8 Kbps for about $1 per hour. Users are free to use as much of that network bandwidth as they want, and there is no real incentive for them to be frugal with their use of it. The trend for Internet applications is toward more bandwidth-intensive multimedia, voice, and video applications.

There are now proposals being floated advocating a pay-as-you-play model that involves some form of monitoring and metering of the bandwidth used by the Internet user. This switch to metered access might occur as soon as the protocols and support software for access providers are available. This is expected to occur for a number of reasons:

- Network providers will soon need to be in a position to be able to guarantee bandwidth and quality of service to business customers.

- Internet users will push for a quality and reliability model, similar to that which they currently enjoy with their existing telephone service. For example, when users reach for the telephone for normal or emergency purposes, they always get a dial tone, even if the electric power is out.

It is anticipated that the Internet will follow the current telecommunications network model consisting of long distance carriers (such as AT&T, MCI, and Sprint) and access providers (such as Pacific Bell, NYNEX, Bell Atlantic, Bell South, and Bell Canada). Big ISPs will provide the means for smaller ISPs to provide global access for their customer base.

Internet cooperatives are likely to be established that will provide at-cost facilities for member companies. As metered charging starts being rolled out, or as businesses start to rely more heavily on the Internet for critical business traffic carriage, small business-oriented underlay networks are likely to develop to service the heavy traffic demands that will exist between large cities, in much the same way as MCI entered the long distance business by setting up shop between a few large cities.

g. *Internet access*

Continued demand for Internet access and network bandwidth is expected. It is likely that some of the regional ISPs will be absorbed by larger networks in an industry shakeout. These larger businesses will be looking to rapidly increase market share and capacity. However, even with big business at work, small regional ISPs or BBSs will probably not disappear. In fact, it is likely that the two will merge to provide a confederation of enhanced services.

Access software tools are expected to continue to mature and become easier to use. As with most maturing software tools, they will grow in size to consume hard disk space and memory, requiring top-end PCs in order to use them effectively. On the positive side, the freeware and shareware software that supports the Internet is likely to continue to mature and alleviate the need for users to purchase any access software, unless they really want to.

ISDN access, which will provide up to 128 Kbps to the home, is expected to increase in its penetration. Cost is also expected to drop and become more consistent as the number of users of the service increases. This access method will provide a connection capability supporting high-speed applications such as video conferencing and multimedia applications.

h. *Regulatory influences*

Government regulation and policies are expected to increase and solidify as the Internet is brought on as a key component of the information highway infrastructure. In the United States, there is great concern about encryption and the security of information and financial data. In both the United States and Canada, there is concern about the uncontrolled nature of the content on the Internet, in particular pornography. It is possible, with the global reach of the Internet, for individuals in one country to unknowingly break the laws of others. Continued legal actions and precedents will gradually stabilize law in cyberspace.

i. *Telecommunications and cable television-based broadband Internet*

Telecommunications providers and the cable television companies are developing equipment called *set top boxes* that will allow a host of new high-capacity services, including home shopping, video on demand, video telephony, interactive games, and home banking, to be offered in the home. These current technologies will be expensive and will take some time to penetrate into the consumer market.

It is also clear that the provision of increased video services to both business and the consumer is the direction of the computer, telecommunications, cable television, and entertainment companies over the next five years. The direction bodes well for the business that is already operating on the Internet, since a high-capacity Internet is a natural extension of the existing market.

These are the many trends which will continue over the next five years and cause the business environment to change with them. A business that tracks these trends will be able to profit from the change itself.

Appendix
Recommended Reading

With the rising public interest in the Internet, there has been a flood of books and material on every possible aspect of the subject. We feel that the following references are good places to start your research on the Internet.

a. Books

1. Internet history

If you want more details about the Internet's technical background and history, this is the definitive book.

> Quarterman, John S. *The Matrix: Computer Networks and Conferencing Systems Worldwide*. Burlington, MA: Digital Press, 1990.

2. Internet tools

If you want a more detailed understanding of the Internet tools, these books will be of help.

> December, John and Neil Randall. *The World Wide Web Unleashed*. Indianapolis: Sams Publishing, 1994.
>
> Gregory, Kate and Noel Estabrook. *Using UseNet Newsgroups: The User-Friendly Reference*. Indianapolis: Que Corporation, 1994.
>
> Krol, Ed. *The Whole Internet User's Guide*, special edition. Sebastopol, CA: O'Reilly and Associates, 1994.
>
> Levine, John R. and Carol Baroudi. *Internet Secrets*. Foster City, CA: IDG Books Worldwide, 1995.
>
> *The Internet Unleashed*. Indianapolis: Sams Publishing, 1994.

3. On-line marketing

The book to read if you want to look at on-line marketing with more of a slant toward using commercial OSPs.

> Janel, Daniel S. *On-line Marketing Handbook: How to Sell, Advertise, Publicize, and Promote Your Products and Services on the Internet and Commercial On-line Systems.* New York: Van Nostrand Reinhold, 1995.

4. Internet directories

A good reference if you want to find out what's available on the Internet, but prefer to flip through a book rather than on-line directories.

> Maxwell, Christine and Czeslaw Jan Grycz. *New Riders' Official Internet Directory*, 2nd edition. Indianapolis: New Riders Publishing, 1994.

5. Web sites

Planning to develop your own Internet Web site? These books will help get you on the right track.

> Chandler, David M. *Running a Perfect Web Site.* Indianapolis: Que Corporation, 1995.

> Cook, David and Deborah Sellers. *Launching a Business on the Web.* Indianapolis: Que Corporation, 1995.

> Ellsworth, Jill H. and Matthew V. Ellsworth. *Marketing on the Internet: Multimedia Strategies for the World Wide Web.* New York: John Wiley and Sons, 1995.

6. UNIX

If you are interested in setting up your own UNIX-based Internet computer site as the platform for your Internet business, the following references will prove invaluable.

> Eckel, George. *Building a UNIX Internet Server.* Indianapolis: New Riders Publishing, 1995.

> Liu, Cricket, Jerry Peek, Russ Jones, Bryan Buus, and Adrian Nye. *Managing Internet Information Services.* Sebastopol, CA: O'Reilly and Associates, 1994.

7. BBS

If you are considering using traditional BBS technology to implement your Internet business presence, the following two books are good places to start.

> Bryant, Alan D. *Creating Successful Bulletin Board Systems*. Reading, MA: Addison-Wesley, 1993.

> Chambers, Mark L., et al. *Running a Perfect BBS*. Indianapolis: Que Corporation, 1994.

8. Security

Security on the Internet is nothing to take lightly. To find out more details, check out the following books.

> Bacard, Andre. *The Computer Privacy Handbook*. Berkeley: Peachpit Press, 1995.

> Cheswick, William R. and Steven M. Bellovin. *Firewalls and Internet Security: Repelling the Wily Hacker*. Reading, MA: Addison-Wesley, 1994.

> Garfinkel, Simson. *PGP: Pretty Good Privacy*. Sebastopol, CA: O'Reilly and Associates, 1995.

9. Legal issues

More legal information than you can shake a stick at may be found in this book, which highlights legal issues surrounding ISPs and OSPs.

> Rose, Lance. *NetLaw: Your Rights in the Online World*. Berkeley: Osborne McGraw-Hill, 1995.

b. Periodicals

The tremendous interest in Internet has spawned new periodicals aimed at helping the consumer and businessperson make the most of the Internet electronic freeway. In addition, many existing computer-oriented magazines (and even non-computer-oriented magazines and newspapers) have been giving increasing coverage to the Internet. There are magazines to cater to every level of interest and expertise. We have highlighted some of our favorites.

1. Operating your own Internet site

If you are planning to operate your own Internet site, these magazines are for you.

Boardwatch Magazine — Guide to Electronic Bulletin Boards and The Internet.
Boardwatch Magazine.

This magazine provides hard information that you can use. This is one of those few magazines that you will want to read cover to cover.
For subscription information write:
8500 West Bowles Avenue, Suite 210
Littleton, CO 80123
mail to:subscriptions@boardwatch.com

BBS: The Bulletin Board Systems Magazine.
Callers Digest Inc.

For subscription information write:
701 Stokes Road
Medford, NJ 08055
mail to:subscribe@bbsmag.com

2. General Internet magazines

To keep abreast of trends and players in the Internet and on-line community, these magazines are our choice.

Internet World — The Magazine for Internet Users.
Mecklermedia.

For subscription information write:
P.O. Box 713
Mt. Morris, IL 61054
mail to:iwsubs@kable.com

Wired.
Wired Ventures Ltd.

For subscription information write:
520 Third Street, Fourth Floor
San Francisco, CA 94107
mail to:info@wired.com

NetGuide — The Guide to the Internet and On-line Services.
CMP Media.

For subscription information write:
600 Community Drive
Manhasset, NY 11030
mail to:crenta@cmp.com

Online Access — Your Connection to Online Services,
Bulletin Boards and the Internet.
Chicago Fine Print Inc.

For subscription information write:
5615 West Cermak Road
Chicago, IL 60650-9884
mail to:74514.3363@compuserve.com

If you want to keep abreast of new or interesting Internet resources, these magazines will interest you. They also represent a powerful forum for print advertising for their on-line business service. *NetGuide* and *Online Access* both devote a large part of each issue to a categorized listing of interesting and new Internet resources.

c. *Internet*

The Internet itself is a fantastic source of information for the businessperson.

1. For more details on Internet statistics and demographics

- World Wide Web User Survey
  (The Graphics, Visualization and Usability Laboratory
  at Georgia Institute of Technology)
  *http://www.cc.gatech.edu/gvu/user_surveys/User_*
  Survey_Home.html

- NSFNET Statistics (The Graphics, Visualization and
  Usability Laboratory at Georgia Institute of Technology)
  http://www.cc.gatech.edu/gvu/stats/NSF/merit.html

- Yahoo User Survey (Yahoo)
  http://www.yahoo.com/survey/results.html

- Defining the Internet Opportunity Survey
  (O'Reilly and Associates)
  http://www.ora.com/survey/

- NSFNET Backbone Statistics
  ftp://nic.merit.edu/nsfnet/statistics/

- Survey-Net Internet User Polls
  (AccessCom/Progressive Computer Services)
  http://www.survey.net/

- Internet Growth (MIDS)
  http://www.tic.com/mids/growth.html

- Turnpike Demographics (Volant Corp)
  http://turnpike.net/turnpike/demog.html

- Internet Domain Survey (Network Wizards)
  http://www.nw.com/zone/WWW/top.html

- Project 2000 (Vanderbilt University)
  http://www2000.ogsm.vanderbilt.edu/surveys

2. How others do business, or perceive the business opportunities, on the Internet

- CommerceNET
  http://www.commerce.net/information/services/services.html

- Tradewave Galaxy
  http://www.einet.net

- Business Resource Center
  http://www.kcilink.com:80/brc

- The Internet Pearls Index- SoloTech Software
  http://execpc.com:80/~Ewmhogg/bizlinks.html

- GNN Business Pages
  http://gnn.com/gnn/bus/index.html

- First Virtual General Information
  http://www.fv.com

- Cybercash
  http://www.cybercash.com

- IBC: Internet Business Center
  http://www.ibc.com

Glossary

Application

A generic term sometimes used to refer to a computer software program. For example, the word processor on your computer is an application.

Archie

An Internet tool. Users can use the Archie tool to search a database of anonymous FTP files for specific file names or directories.

Archive

A repository of files that may be downloaded to your computer.

Bandwidth

The amount of information which can be transmitted over a communications link. Common computer modems can transfer data at different rates starting at 300 BPS up to 28.8 Kbps. The higher the bandwidth of the communications link, the faster you can receive a file over the computer network.

BBS

Bulletin Board System; typically a PC-based on-line service. BBSs are generally local or regional in their scope of service. The focus is usually on file archives, interactive multiplayer games, and on-line chat conferences. BBSs typically have subscriber bases on the order of hundreds to thousands of subscribers.

Browser

A generic term often used to refer to programs that allow a user to "point-and-click" through Gopherspace or the Web.

CD-ROM

Compact disk, read only memory. The computer equivalent of a music CD. CD-ROMs can hold over 500 Mb of information. To put this in perspective, a typical 3.5-inch floppy disk holds 1.44 Mb of information. CD-ROMs are read only and are generally used to distribute large computer programs, software collections, or information databases.

CGI

Computer gateways interface. This is a standard method that allows Web documents to use programs that are locally resident on the host computer system. This capability allows Web documents to be created on the fly.

Cyberspace

Jargon used to refer to the Internet.

Dial-up

A temporary connection between one computer system and another, usually by dialing the telephone number of the other computer system's modem.

Domain name

Part of the Internet addressing scheme that allows messages to be sent to the correct company or organization that has registered on the Internet. An example of a domain name is "westbury.com," which refers to an organization called Westbury that is registered as a commercial organization. Other types or classifications of organizations include "edu" (educational), "gov" (government), "mil" (military), "net" (administration), and "org" (for all others).

Download

To transfer files from another computer to your own computer.

EDI

Electronic data interchange. EDI supports paperless business transactions between cooperating companies. Business is transacted using electronic forms and computer-to-computer communication.

E-mail

Electronic mail. An electronic message that is passed directly from one user to another using computers — without requiring a postage stamp.

Encryption

The scrambling of a message or file to prevent unauthorized viewing. The message, or file, may be unscrambled using a password or "key."

FAQ

Either a frequently asked question, or a list of the same. Many Usenet newsgroups maintain FAQs to avoid having to answer and re-answer the same questions.

Firewall

A method of protecting your computer system from unauthorized intrusions when connected to the Internet. A necessary precaution if you are connecting your business's computer network to the Internet.

Freeware

On-line software that may be used and distributed without charge.

FTP

File transfer protocol. An Internet tool used for transferring files from one computer to another. Anonymous FTP is a common method of allowing any Internet user using the FTP tool to obtain files from another computer on the Internet without having to be a registered user on that computer. A guest user may log in to a computer using the log-in name "anonymous," and access any files that the system administrator has made public.

Gopher

A menu-based Internet tool used for exploring and accessing Internet resources.

GTRC

Georgia Tech Research Corporation

Hardware

The parts of the computer that you can see and touch, including the visual display terminal, disk drives, central processing unit (CPU), power supply, cables, and other sundry devices associated with the physical make-up of the computer system.

Home page

A top level (i.e., starting point) Web page for a company, organization, or individual. From this location, you can telescope down to get further information, or travel to other sites if the appropriate hypertext links are in place.

Host computer

A computer that may be used by one or more users or applications.

HTML

Hypertext markup language. Generally considered to be the language for writing Web documents. Special sequences of characters and letters allow the user to include references to graphics, sound, images, or other Internet resources — which then may be accessed using a browser by pointing-and-clicking.

HTTP

Hypertext transfer protocol. The standard protocol that a Web browser uses to communicate with a Web site (i.e., Web server). HTTP supports the multimedia capabilities of the Web.

Hypertext

A set of highlighted data in readable text that allows a user to point and click on a particular word to find out more information on the subject. This is a popular method used by computerized help systems that allow the user to create links between information on the system at the user's convenience.

Hytelnet

A computer program available on the Internet. This tool provides a searchable database of Telnet-accessible Internet resources.

Internet

A worldwide collection of computers interconnected by a standard computer-to-computer communications interface generally referred to as TCP/IP. Computers may be temporarily or permanently connected to the Internet.

ISDN

Integrated Services Digital Network. Basic rate ISDN service provides up to 128 Kbps dial-up or dedicated connection between computer systems. ISDN requires special telephone service connections to your home or business in addition to a special ISDN modem.

ISP

Internet service provider; also referred to as Internet access provider or IAP. Any business that provides leased-line or dial-up access to the Internet. An ISP may be a business that specializes in providing Internet access only, or it may provide BBS- and OSP-type services as well.

Jughead

A tool that allows a user to search for information accessible using Gopher.

Kbps

Kilo bits per second. One Kbps is equivalent to 1,000 bits being sent in one second. To put a *bit* in perspective, typically eight bits are required to represent one type-written character. The abbreviation *Kbps* is used extensively to refer to modem and leased-line capacities.

Leased-line

A dedicated telephone line connection between one location and another.

Linux

A freeware operating system for PCs offering features comparable to commercial UNIX operating systems. It is interesting to note that Linux is a collaborative effort of many programmers working simultaneously around the world who are using the Internet to let them work as a team, regardless of physical location.

Mailbot

An electronic mail-handling software program that can automatically process e-mail sent to a specific e-mail address without human intervention.

Modem

A device used to allow one computer to communicate with another over the telephone line. Modems are available for a variety of communication speeds, currently ranging between 2.4 Kbps to 28.8 Kbps. The higher the speed, the less time you spend waiting.

Moderated newsgroup or mailing list

All newsgroup or e-mail messages are reviewed by an individual, referred to as the "moderator," to filter out off-topic messages before being posted to the associated mailing list or newsgroup.

Multimedia

A combination, or integration, of various media, such as graphics, video, audio, and text.

NCSA

National Center for Supercomputer Applications

Newsgroups

Usenet discussion groups. Usenet currently has over 10,000 newsgroups ranging from the serious to the banal.

NSF

National Science Foundation. The organization that managed the Internet backbone in the United States until 1995.

On-line

Jargon referring to users being connected to the Internet or other computer services such as those provided by BBSs and OSPs.

OSP

On-line service provider. On-line services typically have extensive information databases or services available in addition to BBS-type services. Generally national or international in their scope of service, OSPs typically have subscriber bases ranging from tens of thousands to millions of subscribers.

PC

Personal computer (usually referring to computers which use Microsoft DOS or Windows operating systems).

PDF

Portable document format. A standard file format that allows documents to be viewed and printed on a large variety of different computer types, for example, Macintoshes or PCs.

PGP

Pretty good privacy. An encryption tool that allows messages and files to be kept secure from unauthorized viewing.

Post

On-line posting is the equivalent of pinning a message on a bulletin board at the grocery store.

PPP

Point to point protocol. A method of connecting your PC to a host Internet computer.

Prodigy

An on-line service owned by IBM and Sears.

Protocol

A specifically defined method that allows two computer programs, or two persons, to communicate in a specific way. For example, FTP is a protocol that defines how software programs can transfer files between any two computers.

RAM

Random access memory. Computer memory that is used to store computer program software and data associated with the computer program. This memory is volatile and any information that is stored in this area is erased once the computer power is turned off.

Real time

The relative speed of processing information on a computer system. A video conferencing system, for example, must process the incoming video pictures of the video conferencing participants as the participants are talking to allow for the natural interaction of participants. The telephone network must process the human voice in real time to allow for "real time" human interaction as well. Real time computer processing is usually measured in microseconds or milliseconds. Examples of non-real time computer activities include searching a large database which might take minutes or hours.

RFC

Request for comment. Refers to documents that define the standards that computers must support to access and use the Internet. RFC documents also include recommended practices or guidelines for computer users.

SATAN

A freeware program that tests the security integrity of Internet computers.

Secure transactions

The passing of information (such as credit card or personal information) between computer applications (such as Web browsers and Web sites) that is encrypted to prevent unauthorized interception.

Server

An application residing on a computer system that provides information to one or more users. A Web site is considered a server since it provides the information (e.g., Web pages and graphics files) requested by Web browsers.

Shareware

Software that may be used and distributed. Users are generally expected to pay a charge to the author after an evaluation period if they want to continue using the software.

Shell

A type of account, usually password protected, that is provided for dial-up users to access the Internet. Usually a text-only interface with no multimedia capabilities.

Signature or .sig

A short note (three to six lines) usually attached to the end of an e-mail or newsgroup message that contains your name, address, and other information about you or your business.

SLIP

Serial line Internet protocol. A method of connecting your PC to a host Internet computer.

Software

Specific computer applications that allow a user to perform tasks, including word processing, creating spreadsheets or drawings using computer-aided drafting, creating or modifying graphics, or roaming the Internet. Software is created using various programming languages, and is sold for specific computer hardware systems, including PCs, engineering workstations, and mainframes.

Spamming

Posting advertising or off-topic messages to one or more unrelated Usenet newsgroups.

System administrator

A person with special computer skills and authority who sets up users, computer resources, and security measures (including passwords and user IDs) on a given computer system. This person also ensures users are not abusing the particular computing resources.

Telnet

An Internet tool that allows you to log in to another computer system on the Internet without having to dial up the system.

Transparent

When the underlying complexity is hidden from the user, such as when a user connects from his or her computer to another computer without needing to know the specific details of the network in between. Graphical user interfaces using point-and-click methods have removed much of the drudgery of having to remember long sequences of commands to connect across the network.

UNIX

A widely used operating system on the Internet. UNIX is generally more complex to set up and maintain than PC operating systems such as DOS and Windows NT.

URL

Uniform resource locator. A standard method of specifying the address of a resource on the Internet that a user wants to access.

Usenet

User Network. A large conferencing system that uses the Internet to distribute its newsgroups. Usenet consists of over 10,000 newsgroups. Newsgroups are the equivalent of special interest groups. A user may select any newsgroup and view all messages that have been posted. Users may also post messages to newsgroups.

Veronica

A tool that allows a user to search for information accessible using Gopher.

Virtual storefront

A computer location on the Internet, typically a Web site, that allows users to peruse a company's goods in the form of an electronic catalogue, as well as electronically order the goods. Virtual storefronts may be located in virtual malls or they may stand alone, without the aid of the electronic mall operator.

WAIS

Wide area information server. An Internet tool used for accessing databases available via the Internet.

Web

World Wide Web. Also referred to as WWW. A hypertext system for locating and accessing Internet resources.

WWW

World Wide Web. See "Web."